Better Homes and Gardens®

crafting with 4 supplies

make it simple

Meredith® Books
Des Moines, Iowa

Make It Simple—Crafting with 4 Supplies
Editor: Carol Field Dahlstrom
Writer: Susan M. Banker
Designer: Lyne Neymeyer
Copy Chief: Terri Fredrickson
Copy and Production Editor: Victoria Forlini
Editorial Operations Manager: Karen Schirm
Managers, Book Production: Pam Kvitne, Marjorie J. Schenkelberg, Rick von Holdt
Contributing Copy Editor: Diane Doro
Contributing Proofreaders: Julie Cahalan, Karen Grossman, Sara Henderson
Photographers: Andy Lyons Cameraworks, Meredith Photo Studio
Photostyling Assistant: Donna Chesnut
Technical Illustrator: Shawn Drafahl
Editorial and Design Assistants: Kaye Chabot, Mary Lee Gavin, Karen McFadden
Project Designers: Heidi Boyd, Kristen Deitrich, Phyllis Dunstan, Ginny McKeever, Alice Wetzel
Technical Assistant: Judy Bailey

Meredith® Books
Editor in Chief: Linda Raglan Cunningham
Design Director: Matt Strelecki
Executive Editor, Food and Crafts: Jennifer Dorland Darling

Publisher: James D. Blume
Executive Director, Marketing: Jeffrey Myers
Executive Director, New Business Development: Todd M. Davis
Executive Director, Sales: Ken Zagor
Director, Operations: George A. Susral
Director, Production: Douglas M. Johnston
Business Director: Jim Leonard

Vice President and General Manager: Douglas J. Guendel

Better Homes and Gardens® **Magazine**
Editor in Chief: Karol DeWulf Nickell

Meredith Publishing Group
President, Publishing Group: Stephen M. Lacy
Vice President-Publishing Director: Bob Mate

Meredith Corporation
Chairman and Chief Executive Officer: William T. Kerr

In Memoriam: E.T. Meredith III (1933–2003)

All of us at Meredith® Books are dedicated to providing you with information and ideas to create beautiful and useful projects. We welcome your comments and suggestions. Write to us at: Meredith Books, Crafts Editorial Department, 1716 Locust Street—LN112, Des Moines, IA 50309-3023.

If you would like to purchase any of our crafts, cooking, gardening, home improvement, or home decorating and design books, check wherever quality books are sold. Or visit us at: bhgbooks.com

Cover Photograph: Andy Lyons Cameraworks

Only Four Supplies?

Every time I go to the crafts store I am pleasantly overwhelmed with all the choices of things to buy. I love the colors of the clay, the patterns of the papers, the shapes and sparkles of the beads, the sheer beauty of the ribbons, the glorious hues of the paints, and the rows and rows of products that seem to multiply every time I shop. And of course I buy all kinds of things that I must have—like colored bells, all shapes of mirrors, spools of colored wire, handfuls of metallic floss, yards of embroidered ribbon, and tiny pieces of foam in fun shapes. I just love to own such inspiring products and have them close at hand—even though I may not have a plan for them yet!

It doesn't always take a plethora of products to create a wonderful project. In this book each chapter offers ideas using only four supplies and every chapter offers you a new challenge. You'll be amazed at what you can make—you'll find elegant clay finials, ribboned greeting cards, flower pot picture holders, paper Christmas ornaments, contemporary coasters, and so much more.

So if you have a sampling of every possible craft product or if you just want to buy a few supplies to get started, you'll have fun creating clever crafts using your talent and only four supplies.

Carol Field Dahlstrom

table of contents

8

32

58

80

106

130

How to use this book

So few supplies...so much to make!

Crafters often say they want more ideas for the crafts supplies they purchase. This book offers dozens of ideas using favorite crafts supplies.

Deciding on the supplies for each chapter and then creating the projects themselves was a fun test. It was amazing to see the many different ways we could interpret the challenge. The outcome? Page after page of very different designs that all use the same four supplies devoted to the chapter.

You'll know the main supplies at a glance.

Each chapter begins with a listing of the supplies used in that chapter. Each item in the list is also accompanied by a symbol (like this ✎ for acrylic paints) that appears in the materials list. Some projects use all four of the chapter supplies, and other projects use only some of them. The supplies for each chapter include the following:

- **Chapter 1**
  Polymer Clay
  Colored Wire
  Beads
  Buttons

- **Chapter 2**
  Colored Card Stock
  Stickers
  Marking Pens
  Glitter

- **Chapter 3**
  Air-Dry Clay
  Acrylic Paints
  Glitter
  Crafts Foam

- **Chapter 4**
  Scrapbook Papers
  Ribbons
  Rubber Stamps and Pads
  Marking Pens

- **Chapter 5**
  Beads
  Elastic Cord
  Glass Votive Candleholders
  Glass Paints

- **Chapter 6**
  Clay Flowerpots
  Acrylic Paints
  Marking Pens
  Polymer Clay

Gather basic supplies to use over and over!

Most of the crafts projects also include basic supplies that you most likely have around the house, such as:

- thick white crafts glue
- scissors
- tape
- tracing paper
- pencils
- tools
- paintbrushes

If a project uses any of the basic supplies, they are listed at the end of the materials list so you can have them handy. Look for a ✛ symbol by the listing.

Occasionally a project lists an "optional" supply, such as a glaze for sheen or protection. You can decide if you want to use this product on your craft.

What craft will you come up with?

Go ahead and get crafting! You'll be amazed at what fun you can have using the same group of four supplies!

Chapter 1

Chapter 2

Chapter 3

Chapter 4

Chapter 5

Chapter 6

Polymer Clay
Colored Wire
Beads
Buttons

Grab your favorite colors of 🧱 , some ◎ to wrap and twist, a handful of sparkling 🫘 , and a variety of 🔘 to make clever crafts for you *and* your home!

Posy Purse

Sitting on a table or hanging on the wall, this pretty clay purse makes a clever holder for a silk or dried bouquet.

Polymer Clay
- 3 squares in 3 colors

Colored Wire
- three 17-inch-long pieces in 3 colors

Beads
- blue seed

Button
- large

+ Basic Supplies
- tracing paper; pencil
- rolling pin; crafts knife
- ruler; fork; toothpick
- paper towel; glue

Here's how

1 Trace the patterns, *opposite;* cut out. On a flat work surface, use a rolling pin to flatten one square of polymer clay to approximately ⅛-inch thickness and large enough to accommodate the purse front pattern. Place the pattern on the clay and use a knife to cut out the shape.

2 Using half a square of another color, roll a piece large enough for the purse flap. Cut around the pattern. Gather the leftover scraps and roll into a piece large enough to cut out five ½-inch strips. Cut a small scrap from the purse front clay into a long narrow strip. Lay this along the curved side of the flap. Use the tines of a fork to push the strip in place.

3 Lay the strips and flap on top of the purse. Cut off the excess strip ends. Gently press the strips and flap onto the purse. Use a toothpick to poke a hole in each top corner of the purse.

4 From the third square of clay, roll a piece large enough to cut out the purse back. From clay scraps make three small balls and flatten to form circles. Press them onto the first, third, and fifth strips on the purse front.

5 Crumple up a paper towel and place on the center of purse back. Lay the purse front over the paper towel, lining up the edges of the front and back pieces. Gently press and smooth edges together.

6 Bake the clay according to the manufacturer's directions.

7 Braid three pieces of colored wire, leaving 2½ inches at the ends. Slip the end of one of the three wires through the hole punched in the purse front. Wrap the ends of the other two wires around the third wire, leaving 2 inches of the third wire free. Finish by twisting the end of the wire around the top of the loop under the other two wrapped wires. Repeat for the other end of the handle.

8 Glue beads down the center of the second and fourth strips and along the top edge of the purse. Glue a button on the flap.

Purse Back Pattern

Purse Front Pattern

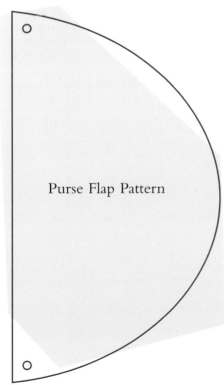

Purse Flap Pattern

Wearable Art

Geometric shapes and intricate details make these clay pendants miniature works of art.

 Polymer Clay
- black, white, and 2 desired colors

 Colored Wires
- medium- and lightweight gauge wire

 Beads
- decorative glass beads

 Basic Supplies
- waxed paper
- rolling pin
- plastic knife
- small paintbrush
- wire cutters
- round-nose pliers
- glass baking dish

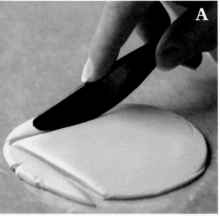

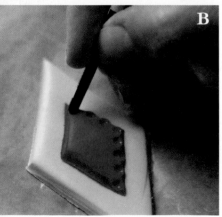

Here's how

1 *For the diamond necklace,* place one-fourth square of clay between sheets of waxed paper. Roll to ⅛ inch thick. Use a plastic knife to cut a long diamond shape from the clay as shown in Photo A.

2 Roll a piece of contrasting clay and cut a small diamond it. Press in the center of the large diamond. Use a paintbrush handle to add texture around the edge of the small diamond as shown in Photo B.

3 Roll marble-size balls from both black and white clay. Shape each into a long rope. Twist the ropes together until the twisted rope is long and narrow. Make a small loop in the center and press against the bottom of the diamond shape. Gently press the rope ends up each side of the diamond; coil the ends where they meet.

4 Roll a pea-size piece of black clay and a smaller piece of colored clay. Press the small clay ball in the center of the black ball and press both into the center of the small diamond shape.

5 Add a contrasting clay rope on the outside edges, coiling the ends at the bottom. Cut a 1½-inch piece of medium-weight wire. Use round-nose pliers to curl one end. Thread a bead or two on the wire and press the straight end into the top of the diamond.

6 *For the intertwined necklace,* create several sizes and colors of ropes as described in Step 3, *above.* Shape the largest coil first and then position the remaining coils as desired.

7 Cut a 1½-inch piece of medium-weight wire. Use round-nose pliers to curl one end. Press the straight end into the top of the clay, adding a bead between the ropes if desired.

8 For both necklaces, place the clay pieces on a glass baking dish and bake them in the oven according to the clay manufacturer's directions. To wear, string pendants on lightweight wire or cording.

Charming St. Nick

Curls of clay make this Santa seem happy from the top of his hat to the tip of his beard.

Polymer Clay
- beige, white, dark red, green, and black

Colored Wire
- 1½-inch piece of medium weight

+ Basic Supplies
- glass baking dish

Here's how

1 Shape a golf ball-size piece of beige clay into an oval and flatten until the shape is approximately ½ inch thick. Place the oval in the center of the baking dish.

2 For the nose, roll two pea-size beige balls and one slightly larger ball. Press a smaller ball on each side of the larger one. Position the nose in the center of the oval.

3 Using half a golf ball-size piece of red clay, shape a ½-inch-thick triangle. Pull and shape one triangle point to form the hat tip. Bend the tip slightly to the left. Place the hat on one end of the oval and press together.

4 For the hat brim, roll a piece of white clay into a 3-inch-long cylinder, approximately the diameter of a pencil. Roll the ends into points. Shape the piece into an arch. Form each end into a small coil. Press the shape firmly over the area where the hat meets the oval.

5 Make a large white coil for the tip of the hat. Make small white coils for the beard, mustache, and eyebrows, noting the shapes for each in the photo, *opposite*. Make three small green coils for the hat embellishments. Press the coils in place.

6 For the eyes, roll two tiny black ovals. Press into place just above the nose.

7 Bend the wire into a U shape. Push the ends into the top of the hat, leaving a small loop for the hanger.

8 Bake the clay in the oven according to the manufacturer's instructions. Let cool.

Color-Splashed Beads

Combine swirled and layered clay beads to make funky one-of-a-kind necklaces.

 Polymer Clay
• desired colors

 Colored Wire
• fine beading wire

Beads
• small

+ Basic Supplies
• Phillips screwdriver, decorative-edge scissors, toothpick, or other items to create texture in clay
• glass baking dish

Here's how

1 Create multitone beads by rolling, twisting, and blending two colors together, such as green and yellow or turquoise and green. Experiment with the clay until the blended colors are pleasing. The more the clay is worked, the more blended the colors will become.

2 Shape a bead by rolling a small amount of clay in your hands until it becomes soft and smooth. Roll it into a ball or an oval. Shape a triangular-shaped log and then slice it into pieces. The clay can also be formed into blocks or disk shapes by rolling pieces into balls and pressing as flat as desired.

3 To add texture to a bead, roll small balls of clay and press onto the bead. Roll a smaller ball and press onto the first ball to create a dot.

4 Add texture by using the end of a Phillips screwdriver, a toothpick, or another tool.

5 To make a twisted bead, roll two different colors of clay into long smooth strands. Twist the strands together and then roll them around a toothpick. Remove the toothpick.

6 Use a toothpick to make holes in the beads. Move it around the inside of the hole to make it larger if needed. Check to be sure the wire will fit through the holes before you bake the clay beads.

7 Place the beads in a glass baking dish and bake in the oven according to the manufacturer's instructions.

8 Let the beads cool. String the beads onto beading wire, alternating with purchased beads. Knot the wire ends.

Cute-As-A-Clown Hook

The smiles will be contagious when you hang your hat next to this happy-go-lucky fellow!

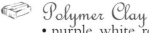 **Polymer Clay**
- purple, white, red, pink, and yellow

Colored Wire
- green, purple, orange, and yellow

 Beads
- black seed
- green small tube

+ Basic Supplies
- ruler
- toothpick
- baking sheet
- small blocks of wood
- pencil
- rolling pin
- wire cutters
- thick white crafts glue
- wood-back coatrack, screws, and screwdriver

Here's how

1 For the hook roll half a square of purple clay to a 6½-inch tapered rope. Flatten 2 inches of the larger end to a ¾-inch width. Use a toothpick to make two holes for hanging and shape into a hook. Place the clay on a baking sheet with the top of the hook between blocks of wood to keep the back straight while baking. Bake according to the manufacturer's directions. Cool; set aside.

2 For the clown head use one-fourth of the white clay square; roll it into a ball. Use the end of a pencil to poke a hole in the bottom. Widen the hole to fit over the narrow end of the hook. Add a small red clay ball for a nose. Flatten two tiny balls of pink clay for cheeks. Push beads into place for the eyes and mouth. Set aside.

3 For the hat divide a ¾-inch ball of orange clay in half and roll each into balls. Flatten one ball for the brim and shape the other into the hat top. Press the top on the brim and smooth the edges. Wrap a contrasting strip of clay around the hat. Press the hat gently on top of the head. Use the end of a piece of wire to poke ¼-inch-deep holes on each side of the head close to the hat brim.

4 For the collar roll out a 2-inch circle, trimming away any excess. Set the head on top of the collar and make a hole in the collar to correspond to the hole in the head. Flute the edges of the collar.

5 Slip the head with collar and hat onto the narrow end of the hook. Roll a small rope and place it around the hook and under the collar. Smooth the edges of the rope into the collar and hook.

6 Place the hook, flat side down, on a baking sheet. Bake using blocks of wood to prop up the curved end of hook. Let cool.

7 Cut colored wire into 6-inch pieces and twist into curls. Dip one end of each wire in glue and insert into the holes in the head. Let dry. Attach the hook to the coatrack backing using screws or nails.

Light Catcher

Let the lamplight shine through a chain of glistening beads.

 **Polymer Clay**
- purple

Colored Wire
- 24-inch length purple

Beads
- assorted glass and crystal; crimp

Buttons
- 2 vintage purple

+ **Basic Supplies**
- pencil; baking sheet

Here's how

1 With purple polymer clay make a flat, circular pendant approximately 1½ inches in diameter. Carve a design in the pendant and write an inspirational word on the back if desired. With the tip of a pencil, make a hole at the top large enough for two wires to pass through. Follow the clay manufacturer's directions to bake the pendant in the oven.

2 Fold the wire in half and thread the folded end through the hole in the clay pendant. Bring the wire ends through the loop and gently pull to secure.

3 Thread approximately eight small beads on both wires in the same order. Thread the two wires through a larger bead to create an oval shape.

4 Thread more beads on the separate wires. Again string the two wires through a larger bead to form a second oval.

5 Add one button, a small bead, and the other button. Leave a loop for hanging; then twist the wire tightly and cut off the excess. If desired use a crimp bead instead of twisting the wire.

All-Buttoned-Up Candles

Surround a pillar candle with zigzags of wire and buttons of all kinds.

Here's how

1 Place a cup hook in the drill and tighten. Bend an 80-inch length of wire in half. Place the loop over the cup hook. Secure the wire ends in a vise. Pulling firmly on the drill, turn it on to twist the wire. Remove from cup hook.

2 Bend the wire back and forth to the height of the candle. When the bent wire will wrap around the candle, cut the wire. Secure the ends together. Glue buttons onto wire as desired. Let dry. Slip the candle inside the ring.

Colored Wire
• desired color

Buttons
• assorted

+ Basic Supplies
• small cup hook
• drill
• wire cutter
• vise
• pillar candle
• hot-glue gun
• glue sticks

Clever Clay Coasters

Embedded buttons, beads, and wire make artwork out of clay slabs.

 **Polymer Clay**
• desired colors

Colored Wire
• 20-gauge metallic

Beads
• assorted

Buttons
• assorted

+ Basic Supplies
• rolling pin
• waxed paper
• crafts knife
• tracing paper and pencil (optional)
• needle-nose pliers
• wire cutters
• glass baking dish
• glaze, such as Sculpey (optional)
• paintbrush

Here's how

1 Place the clay between two pieces of waxed paper and flatten with a rolling pin.

2 Fold and stack the clay. Press down gently to remove air pockets. Cut out 3½-inch squares or 4-inch circles using a crafts knife. (If desired trace the circle, *below,* to use as a pattern.)

3 Snip off shanks of buttons. Bend small pieces of gold wire into shapes. Press buttons, wire, and beads into clay. Bake according to the manufacturer's directions.

4 If desired, brush the coaster surface with glaze for protection.

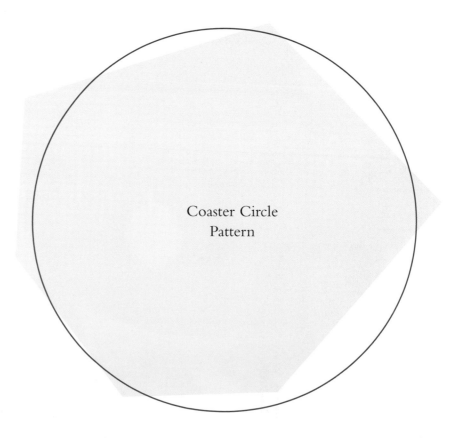

Coaster Circle
Pattern

Beaded Candle Collars

Embellish clay shapes with wire and beads to encircle taper candles with romantic flair.

 **Polymer Clay**
• desired colors

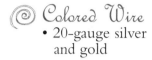 **Colored Wire**
• 20-gauge silver and gold

 **Beads**
• assorted

+ Basic Supplies
• rolling pin
• waxed paper
• crafts knife
• cookie cutters (optional)
• round-nose pliers
• wire cutters
• glaze, such as Sculpey (optional)

Here's how

1 Place the clay between two pieces of waxed paper and roll it flat with a rolling pin.

2 Fold and stack the clay. Press down gently to remove air pockets. Cut out various shapes of clay using a crafts knife or use cookie cutters in desired shapes. Cut a circle out of the center of the clay collar for the candle to pass through.

3 Press beads as desired onto the clay candle collar. Plan where wire holes need to be and insert small pieces of scrap wire before baking the clay. Bake according to the manufacturer's directions. Let cool. Apply a coat of glaze for protection if desired.

4 Cut wire for candle collars and coil one end of each wire using round nose pliers. Thread wires through holes. Add beads and coil the other end of each wire.

Clay Napkin Rings

Create sparkling napkin rings that make any occasion special.

 Polymer Clay
- desired colors

 Colored Wire
- 20-gauge gold

 Beads
- assorted, small tube and rochelle

✚ Basic Supplies
- rolling pin
- waxed paper
- crafts knife
- paper towel tube (optional)
- wire cutters
- round-nose pliers
- glass baking dish

Here's how

1 Use a rolling pin to flatten the clay between two pieces of waxed paper.

2 Fold and stack the clay. Press down gently to remove air pockets. Cut out a strip of clay 1¾ inch wide using a crafts knife. Wrap clay around cardboard tube and press clay ends together; cut away the excess. (Or trace the rectangle, *below,* for a pattern.)

3 Press small glass tube beads around the edges of napkin ring. If desired, string small glass rochelle beads on wire, coil into shapes, and press into clay. Bake according to the manufacturer's directions.

4 Wrap two pieces of gold wire around center of napkin ring and twist to secure. String beads on wires and coil wire ends with round-nose pliers.

Napkin Ring
Pattern

Clay-Wrapped Beads

Wind glass beads with colorful clay strips to make artsy necklaces everyone will love.

 Polymer Clay
- desired colors

 Colored Wire
- 20-gauge metallic gold

 Beads
- clear glass

+ Basic Supplies
- rolling pin
- waxed paper
- crafts knife
- wire cutters
- round-nose pliers

Here's how

1 Knead each piece of clay with your hands to warm and soften it. To flatten place clay between two pieces of waxed paper and roll flat with a rolling pin.

2 Use a crafts knife to cut thin strips of different colors of clay. Twist strips together. Roll flat and cut very thin strips of blended clay. Wrap clay strips around glass beads, cutting away any excess clay. You can create lines, Xs, swirl designs, or cover the entire bead if desired.

3 Bake the beads in the oven according to the clay manufacturer's directions. Let the beads cool.

4 Cut 3-inch pieces of wire. For each link coil one end of the wire using round-nose pliers, thread a bead on the straight end, and then coil it. Repeat this process and connect the coils to form a necklace.

5 At one end of the necklace, bend a 2-inch piece of wire in half, shape the bend into a hook, and attach to the end of the last coil.

Egg-ceptional Holders

Display natural or decorated eggs in handcrafted clay-stemmed cups.

 ## Polymer Clay
- 3 coordinating colors

+ **Basic Supplies**
  - wooden spoon
  - toothpick
  - glass baking dish
  - newspapers and clear gloss acrylic spray (optional)

Here's how

1 Use a half package of clay and roll it into a ball. Push the end of a wooden spoon into the center to create a hole. Mold a small irregularly shaped bowl large enough to hold an egg.

2 Using other clay colors add decorative dots or thin coils around the bowl. Use a toothpick to texture coils and press to sides of the bowl.

3 Bake the bowl on a baking dish according to the clay manufacturer's directions.

4 For the base roll a nearly full package of clay into a fat tube approximately 1½ inches long. Make a large ball using a little less than half a package of another color. Poke a hole into the center of the ball with wooden spoon handle. Enlarge hole with fingers and insert tube into the hole. Use fingers to smooth edge of ball and tube together. With index finger, flatten the bottom of the ball into an irregular base. Roll a thin coil of contrasting color and wrap around the intersection of the base and the tube.

5 Attach the top of the tube base to the bottom of the bowl by using fingers to smooth tube onto bowl. Allow finger strokes to be a part of the design.

6 Turn eggcup upside down on a baking dish and bake in oven.

7 If desired place the eggcup on newspapers in a well-ventilated work area. Spray the eggcup with clear gloss acrylic spray. Let it dry.

Chapter 2

Colored Card Stock

Stickers

Marking Pens

Glitter

Pick out pretty , go wild with oodles of great , treat yourself to new and , and you're prepared to make some incredible crafts!

Garden Greetings

Just imagine the look of a loved one's face when you present a perfectly wrapped gift.

Colored Card Stock
- green and desired colors

Marking Pens
- to match card stock

Glitter
- gold

+ Basic Supplies
- ruler
- tracing paper
- pencil
- scissors
- spoon
- glue stick
- paper punch

Here's how

1 *For the box bottom* cut a 6¾-inch square from one piece of card stock using the pattern on *page 38*. Lightly draw an X from corner to corner. Fold all sides up to the center of the X. Smooth the folds with the back of a spoon. Refer to the diagram on *page 38* and cut along the dotted lines. Fold up the sides with the flaps on the inside. Glue the flaps in place. *For the box top* cut an 8¼-inch square from a second piece of card stock. Fold the sides in 1¼ inches toward the center. Pinch together the four square corners created by the folds to form triangles, creating the sides of the box at the same time. Glue the inside edges of the triangles together. Punch out dots from card stock and glue to top.

Pink and Yellow Flower

Pink Loop Flower

2 *For all of the flowers* trace the patterns on *pages 36–37;* cut out. Trace around the shapes on card stock and cut out.

3 *For the yellow flower, opposite,* fold and pleat each of the four petals; glue. Glue the petals to the top of a gift box. For the center cut a 1½×2¾-inch strip. Fringe one long edge and roll the strip into a tight tube, gluing the uncut edge. For the shorter fringe cut a 1¼×2¾-inch strip and wrap and glue around the taller fringe. Glue to the flower

center. Outline the leaves and draw veins with a marking pen. Crease along the vein to slightly curve. Glue the leaves to the lid under the flower. Cut out a free-form tendril and glue under the flower. Punch dots and glue randomly across the top and sides of the lid. Let dry.

4 *For the blue flower, below,* outline the two base strips with a matching marking pen. Crisscross the strips and glue in the center. Punch three dots for each strip end; glue in place. Outline the flower shape with matching marking pen. Roll the end of each petal around a pencil to curl toward the center. Glue the flower to the center of the crossed strips. Cut a 1½×2-inch strip and fringe to ¼ inch of long edge. Roll into a tube, gluing the edge as it is rolled. Press the fringe outward; glue the tube to the flower center. Let dry.

5 *For the pink and yellow flower, opposite,* outline the paper pieces with matching marking pens. Glue the smaller flower on the larger one. Cut out a pink oval center, outline, and glue in place. Cut ten short, narrow strips and glue to extend from the flower center. Dot the flower center with glue and sprinkle with glitter. Let dry.

6 *For the pink loop flower, opposite,* cut four ⅜×7-inch strips from bright pink and four from pink. Trace around a quarter twice on white card stock and cut out. Cut nickel-size circles from orange and turquoise. Glue the ends of each of the eight pink strips to the center of one of the white circles like spokes on

a wheel. Make a loop out of each strip and glue to the center. Glue the second white circle in the center. Punch and glue small circles to the top of the light pink petals. Glue the orange and turquoise circles in the flower center. Cut three ¾×6-inch strips from green. Fringe the strips to within ½ inch from one short end. Glue to the back of the flower. Let dry.

continued on page 36

Yellow Flower and Box

Blue Flower

Yellow Flower Leaf
Patterns
(cut one of each)

Pink and Yellow
Flower, and Yellow
Pattern
(cut one for each)

Yellow Flower
Pattern
(cut four)

Pink and Yellow
Flower Pattern
(cut one)

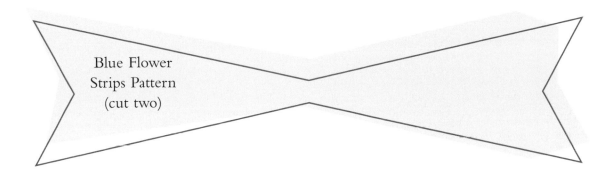

Blue Flower
Strips Pattern
(cut two)

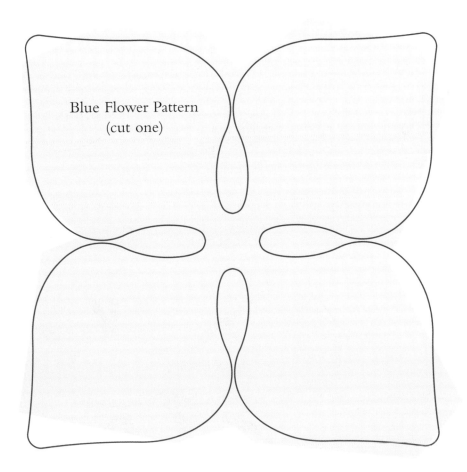

Blue Flower Pattern
(cut one)

(continued on page 38)

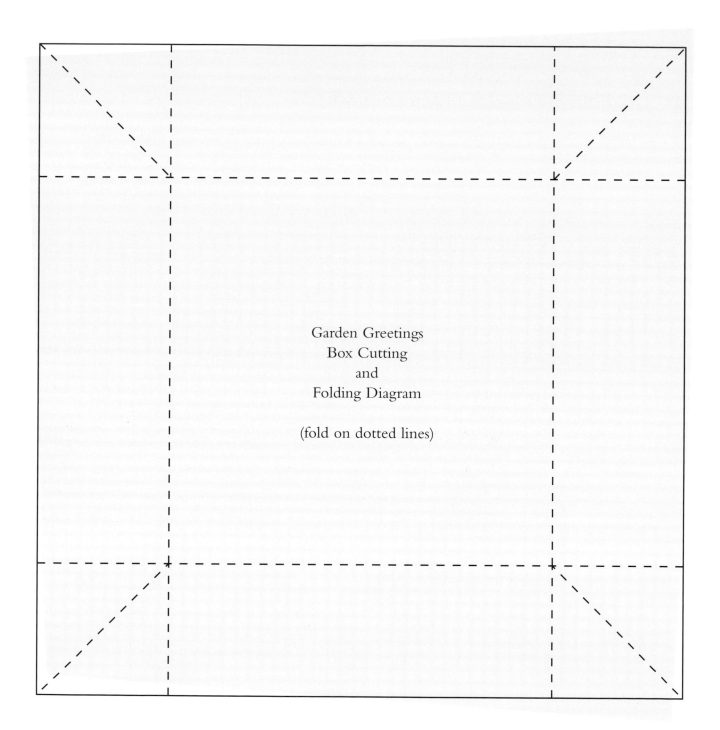

Garden Greetings
Box Cutting
and
Folding Diagram

(fold on dotted lines)

Party Hat Wishes

Use glitter and glue to say happy birthday from you!

Here's how

1 Cut the card stock to the desired card size, allowing for the card to be folded in half. Fold the card in half.

2 Trace the hat pattern, *below*, and cut out. Use the pattern to cut two small triangles from card stock scraps.

3 Cover the hat shapes with crafts glue and sprinkle each hat with a different color of glitter. When dry, shake off excess. Use glue to draw a zigzag line at the bottom of each hat and sprinkle with a contrasting glitter. Shake off excess.

4 Glue hat shapes to card as shown. Use glue to draw lines ¼ inch apart along the bottom and right edge. Sprinkle with glitter. When dry, shake off excess. Use glue to draw lines between the first ones and sprinkle with another color of glitter. Add glitter accents and words to the card front, allowing to dry before starting another color. Let the glue dry.

  Colored Card Stock
• white
• scraps

Glitter
• bright colors

+ Basic Supplies
• tracing paper
• scissors
• pencil
• thick white crafts glue

Hat
Pattern

Big Top Place Cards

This circus parade saves a spot for each kid at the party.

Colored Card Stock
• desired colors

Marking Pens
• black

+ Basic Supplies
• tracing paper; pencil
• scissors
• glue stick

Here's how

1 *For all the animals,* trace the patterns, *pages 42–45.* Cut out the shapes.

2 *For the lion,* fold the background card stock in half. Place the body and head pattern pieces to align with fold; trace around pattern with marking pen; cut out. Draw the face using a marking pen. Outline the orange ears and glue to lion head. Cut out narrow strips from card stock and glue pieces around the lion head for the mane. Open the head and glue the chin to the body on both sides. Glue the tip on tail and glue to the inside edge of one side.

3 *For the elephant,* fold the background card stock in

half. Place the pattern piece to align with fold; trace around piece with marking pen. Cut out. Draw the eye using a marking pen. Cut the foot and ear pieces from a contrasting color; glue in place.

4 *For the zebra,* trace around the pattern on card stock. Cut out the entire body and partial body. Fold the flap to the inside of the partial body. Cut zebra stripes from contrasting colors and glue to the body and neck. Repeat on opposite side of neck and on back of the partial body. Add the eyes, mane, and tail with marking pen. Align and glue corners of partial body to the back of the entire body, leaving the center portion of the flap unglued for banner.

5 For the name, cut a 5×¾-inch-wide strip of paper and notch one end. Write the name on the slip and glue where desired on the paper animal.

continued on page 42

Zebra Front
Place Card Pattern

Zebra Back
Place Card Pattern

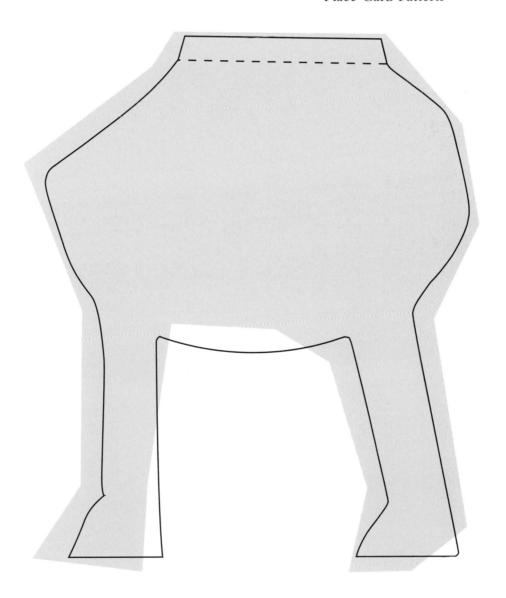

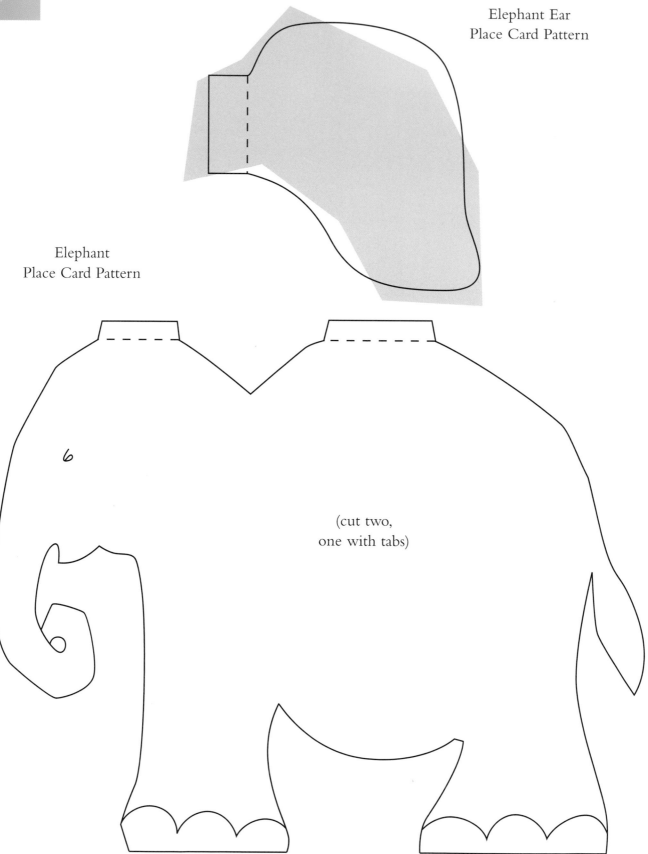

Elephant Ear
Place Card Pattern

Elephant
Place Card Pattern

6

(cut two,
one with tabs)

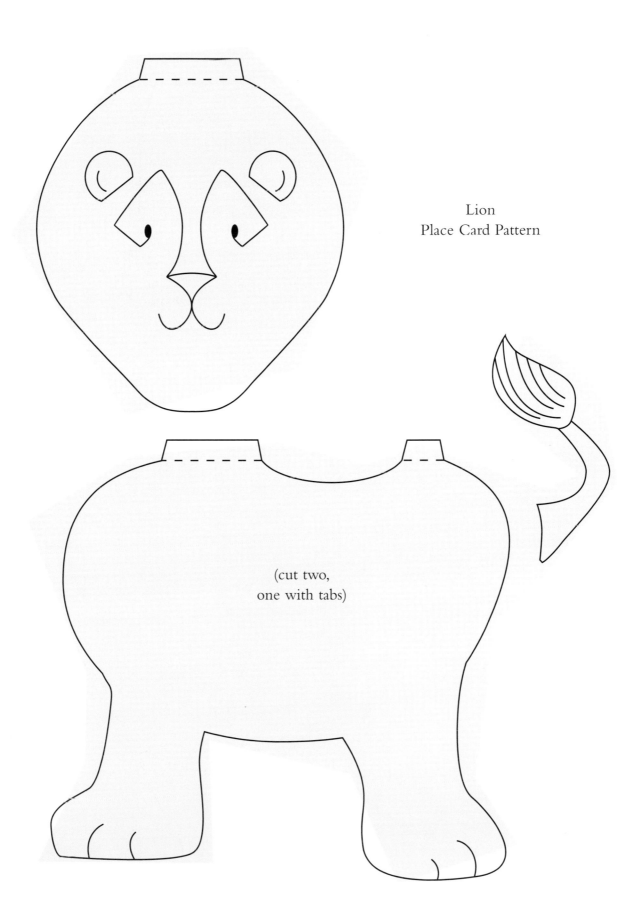

Lion
Place Card Pattern

(cut two,
one with tabs)

Garden Bookmarks

Hold your place in your latest novel with a paper bookmark that's as pretty as a posy.

 Colored Card Stock
- desired colors

 Marking Pens
- green and colors to match card stock

 Glitter
- desired colors of glitter glue

+ Basic Supplies
- tracing paper
- pencil
- scissors
- thick white crafts glue

Here's how

1 Trace the patterns, *below,* and cut out. Use the patterns to cut the stem and leaf shapes. If desired cut veins and a thinner stem from contrasting card stock and glue to the stem.

2 *For the circular flower,* cut various size circles. Cut a zigzag design in the top of one of the inner circles. Outline each circle with a marking pen and glue to the top of the stem. Add glitter dots to the center.

3 *For the petaled flower,* cut petals from two colors of card stock and glue alternating colors in a circle around the top of the stem. Cut two small circles and glue to the center of the petals. Let dry.

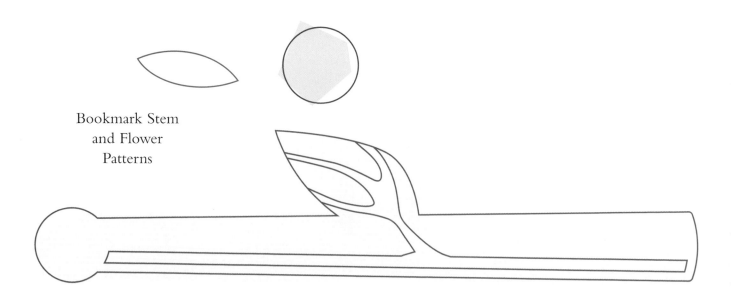

Bookmark Stem
and Flower
Patterns

Tasteful Invites

Make a lasting impression by extending clever invitations to friends and relatives.

 Colored Card Stock
- desired colors

 Stickers
- confetti
- butterfly

 Marking Pens
- medium-tip black

 Glitter
- gold glitter paint in a tube

+ Basic Supplies
- tracing paper
- pencil
- scissors
- paper punch
- thick white crafts glue
- string

Here's how

1 *For the ice cream cone,* trace the patterns, *page 50,* and cut out. Fold a piece of dark yellow card stock in half. Place the bottom of the cone pattern on the fold of the card stock. Trace the cone outline using a black marking pen; cut out. Use a pencil to draw a diagonal grid on the paper cone. Cover the pencil lines with gold glitter paint. Let the paint dry. Glue the side edges together using a narrow line of glue. *For the ice cream,* trace around the patterns on pink card stock; cut out. Write the desired message on the ice cream. Press sticker confetti on the ice cream. Place the paper ice cream in cone. Glue the drips down the cone.

2 *For the teacup,* trace the patterns, *page 51,* and cut out. Trace around the patterns on card stock; cut out. Glue the cup to the saucer. Glue the handle to the cup shape. Cut a slit in the cup. Apply butterfly stickers to the top edge of the cup. Write the desired message on the tea bag. Slip the tea bag into the slot on the cup. *For the tag,* outline the shape in black. Write "tea time" on the tag with a marking pen. Punch a hole at the top center of both the tea bag and the tag. Slip string through the holes and glue in place.

continued on page 50

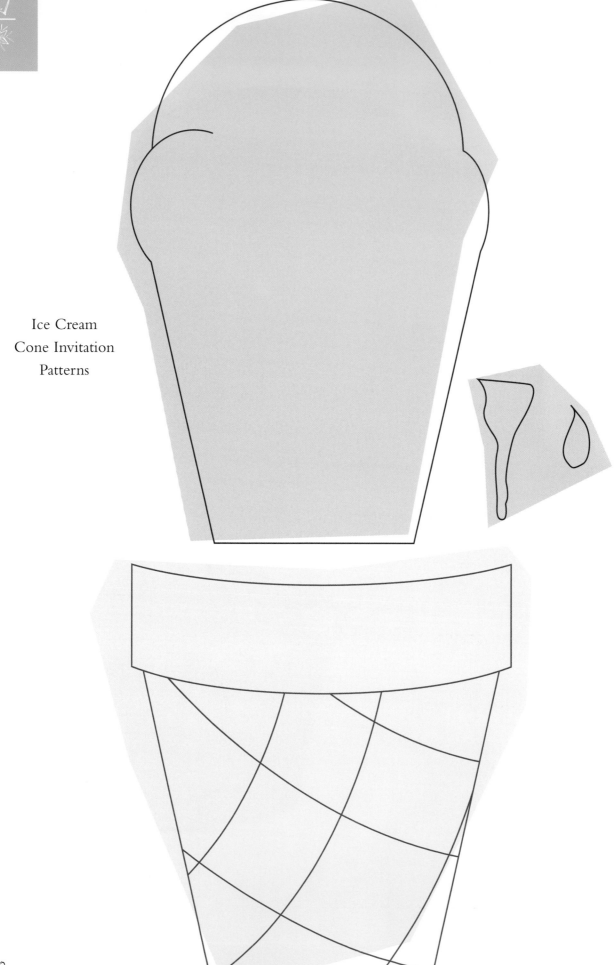

Ice Cream
Cone Invitation
Patterns

Teacup Invitation
Patterns

tea time

Birthday Greetings

Send a birthday card that is both creative and heartfelt.

 Colored Card Stock
- desired colors and patterns

 Stickers
- alphabet and other desired motifs

+ Basic Supplies
- scissors
- decorative-edge scissors
- paper punches in desired shapes
- glue stick

Here's how

1 For each card, cut the background paper to the desired size and fold it in half. Trim the edges of contrasting card stock slightly smaller than the front of the card. You may want to make more than one layer.

2 Punch shapes, such as circles or stars, and add them to any of the paper layers. Adhere the layers together using a glue stick.

3 Place alphabet or motif stickers on the card front. If desired, spell out a greeting using stickers on contrasting paper. Cut out and adhere to the card front.

Photographic Memories

Use a favorite photo to personalize a birthday greeting for a dear friend or relative.

Here's how

1 Crop the photograph as desired using a crafts knife and a ruler. Cut light pink paper to the desired card size, tearing the short edges. Fold it in half.

2 Cut darker pink paper slightly larger than the photo. Tear the edges. Glue the photograph to the dark pink paper. Glue the dark pink paper to the light pink card.

3 Use a gold marking pen to write messages on light pink paper scraps. Cut out and glue to card.

4 Place a sticker in the lower left corner of the card. Apply crafts glue along the torn edge of the card front. Sprinkle with glitter. Let the glue dry.

 Colored Card stock
- shades of pink

 Stickers
- birthday cake

 Marking Pens
- metallic gold

Glitter
- pink

+ **Basic Supplies**
- photograph
- crafts knife
- ruler
- glue stick
- thick white crafts glue

Kitchen Art

In minutes you can make a framable work of art that will perk up your eating area.

 Colored Card Stock
- heavyweight in desired colors

 Stickers
- coffee and alphabet

+ Basic Supplies
- scissors
- frame with mat insert (optional)
- paper punch

Here's how

1 To frame stickers, cut around the desired stickers without removing the backing. Arrange the stickers on a piece of card stock or a mat cut from card stock. Leave an equal space between the stickers to create an organized look.

2 When pleased with the effect, peel off each backing and press stickers into place.

3 To frame, layer the mat over the card stock and insert it into the frame.

4 To embellish a mat, use alphabet stickers to spell words associated with the theme of the stickers. Place the letters horizontally and vertically around the mat.

5 For the tag, spell desired message on card stock using alphabet stickers. Trim a scallop edge around message using scissors. Glue cutout to a contrasting color of cardstock and trim into a rectangle. Round the corners. Punch a hole in one corner and tie to gift with ribbon, wire, or string.

Merry Greeting

Silver stickers in different sizes and fonts combine to make a festive card for the holidays.

 Colored Card Stock
- 5½×9-inch piece of light blue

 Stickers
- alphabet, stars, and dots in silver and white

+ Basic Supplies
- scissors

Here's how

1 Cut the card stock to the desired card size. Fold the card stock in half.

2 Plan the placement of the holiday words and phrases. Starting with the largest letters, peel and press into place. Use the large letters as guides to place small lettering around the words. Fill in the open areas with star and dot stickers using the photo, *below,* for inspiration.

3 If stickers hang over the edge of the card, trim away the excess neatly using scissors.

Traditionally Yours

Use solid and print papers in traditional colors to make a lovely Christmas card.

Here's how

1 Cut a 7×10-inch piece from burgundy card stock; fold. Cut a 6¾×4¾-inch piece from light green; glue to front.

2 Cut a diamond shape from burgundy to fit card. Glue to dark green; trim. Glue on card. Cut a 4¼×2¼-inch piece from beige. Mount on burgundy; trim a narrow border. Mount on medium green; trim. Glue on card. Use stickers to spell "Christmas Greetings" on the card front.

2 Dot glue around edges of card and in diamond. Sprinkle with glitter and let dry. Shake off excess.

 Colored Card Stock
- burgundy, light green print, dark green, beige, and medium green print

 Stickers
- alphabet
- ivy

 Glitter

+ Basic Supplies
- scissors; ruler
- thick white crafts glue
- decorative-edge scissors

Chapter 3

Air-Dry Clay

Acrylic Paints

Glitter

Crafts Foam

When you pick up some easy-to-mold, find in colors you love, shake on shiny, and add accents, you can make great projects!

No-Melt Ice Cream

Create whimsical summertime fun—ice cream cones made of foam and topped with frosty glitter!

Air-Dry Clay
- white

Acrylic Paints
- pale colors

Glitter
- iridescent

Craft Foam
- tan

 Basic Supplies
- tracing paper
- pencil
- scissors
- thick white crafts glue
- paper plate
- stapler
- hot-glue gun
- glue sticks
- paintbrush
- glass tumbler

Here's how

1 Enlarge and trace the cone pattern, *below,* and cut out. Use the pattern to cut the cone shape out of tan craft foam.

2 Lay the cone flat on a protected work surface. Squeeze crafts glue in a diagonal line, from a top corner of the cone down to the bottom of the cone. Repeat the process to create rows of glue ½ inch apart. Make a second set of glue lines starting at the opposite corner and working diagonally down to the bottom of the cone. The crisscross lines should form diamond shapes. Sprinkle the wet glue with iridescent glitter; shake the excess glitter onto a paper plate. Allow the glue to dry completely.

3 Roll up the cone, overlap the edges by a quarter inch, and staple the two layers together. Apply hot glue down the length of the foam edge to glue it flat.

4 Form clay into generous scoops of ice cream and place them into the top of the cone. Let dry.

5 Paint the clay ice cream a pale color and sprinkle iridescent glitter into the wet paint. Stand the cone in a glass tumbler while the paint dries.

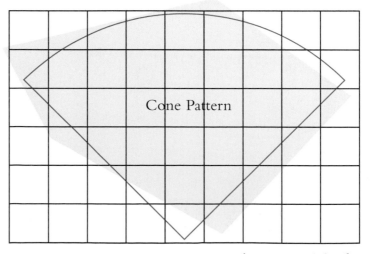

Cone Pattern

1 square=1 inch

Garden-Style Place Mat

Create a stylish floral place mat accented with precut foam letters.

 Craft Foam
- 11½×17-inch piece of dark green
- small sheets of red, medium pink, light pink, medium green, light green, and white
- five 4-inch squares of white
- four 4-inch squares of black
- adhesive letters in red and pink

+ Basic Supplies
- decorative-edge scissors
- ruler
- tracing paper
- pencil
- scissors
- thick white crafts glue
- round paper punch

Here's how

1 Trim the short ends of the dark green rectangle with decorative-edge scissors.

2 Cut two ⅜×11½-inch strips from medium pink foam. Cut two ½×11½-inch strips from medium green foam.

3 Trace the patterns, *opposite,* and cut out. Trace around the shapes on the coordinating colors of craft foam. Cut out 2 large leaves, 18 small leaves, flower centers, and six or 7 petals for each flower. Cut long, narrow S shapes for stems.

4 Glue the white and black squares checkerboard-style in the center of the place mat. Glue a medium pink strip on each side of checkerboard. Glue a medium green strip on each side of the pink strips.

5 Glue the flower and leaf shapes on the mat, using the photo, *below,* for placement.

6 Press foam letters on place mat front, curving around the flower motifs.

7 Punch 12 or more dots from white foam. Glue to black squares in groups of three. Let the glue dry.

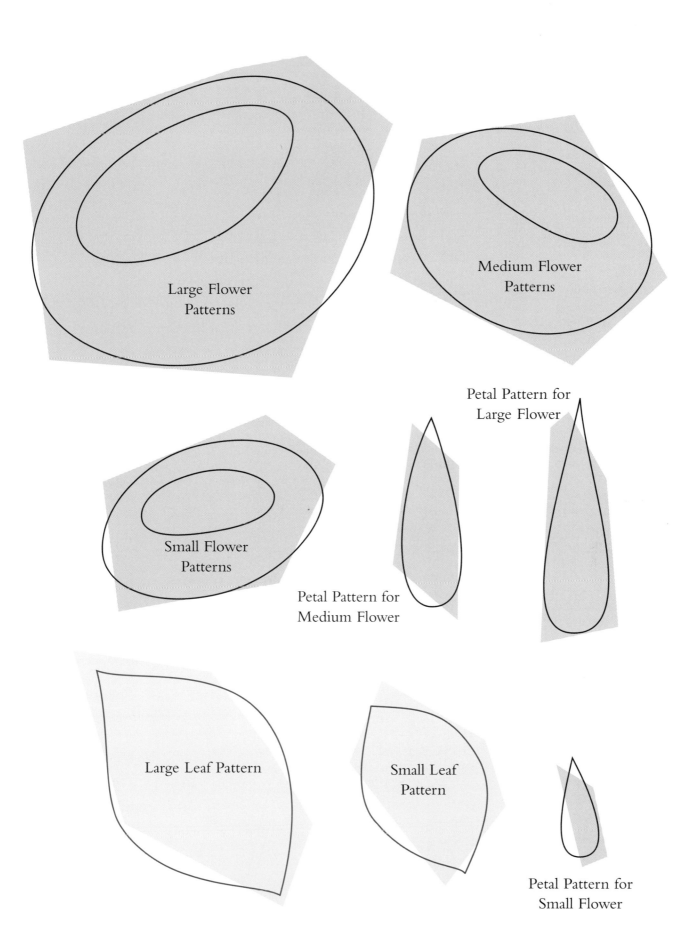

Large Flower
Patterns

Medium Flower
Patterns

Small Flower
Patterns

Petal Pattern for
Large Flower

Petal Pattern for
Medium Flower

Large Leaf Pattern

Small Leaf
Pattern

Petal Pattern for
Small Flower

Miniature Fruit

Fill a fruit bowl with clay versions of Mother Nature's bounty to last season after season.

 **Air-Dry Clay**
- white

 **Acrylic Paints**
- fruit colors and green

 **Craft Foam**
- green

+ Basic Supplies
- pencil
- paintbrush
- clear gloss acrylic spray (optional)
- tracing paper
- scissors

Here's how

1 Shape the clay into apple, pear, banana, plum, cherry, or other fruit shapes using the photo, *opposite,* for inspiration. Use the tip of a pencil to poke a hole into the center top of each fruit if leaves and stems are to be added. Let the clay air-dry according to the manufacturer's directions.

2 Paint the clay fruit. Let the paint dry. If desired coat with clear gloss acrylic spray in a well-ventilated work area.

3 Trace the patterns, *below;* cut out. Trace around the patterns on green craft foam. Cut out the shapes. Accent the leaves with dark green paint. Let the paint dry. Glue each stem into the appropriate hole in the fruit.

Apple Leaf and Stem Pattern

Cherry Leaf and Stem Pattern

Pear Leaf and Stem Pattern

Two-Tone Frame

Create vibrant frames to accommodate any size photo.

 Craft Foam
- desired colors

+ Basic Supplies
- scissors
- ruler
- crafts knife
- paper punches
- thick white crafts glue

Here's how

1 Cut a, 8½×10½-inch piece of craft foam for the outer frame. Round each of the corners if desired. Use one of the corner patterns, *below,* to draw corner slits in all four corners. Cut the slits open with a crafts knife.

2 Decorate the corners with a series of hole punches.

3 Glue the outer frame to an 8×10-inch piece of craft foam for stability.

4 Cut a 7×9-inch piece of black polka-dot craft foam for the front. Cut out the desired opening in the center.

5 Slip the corners of the inside frame under the slits on the outer frame.

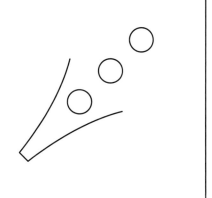

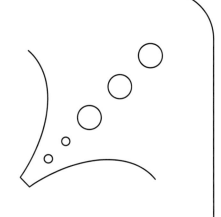

Frame Corner
Patterns

Company Coasters

Set a festive mood at your next gathering with foam coasters that offer a cheerful welcome.

 Acrylic Paints
- in paint pen form in purple, blue, magenta, silver, and gold

 Craft Foam
- black

 Basic Supplies
- tracing paper
- pencil
- scissors

Here's how

1 Trace the pattern, *below,* onto tracing paper. Cut out the shape. Trace around pattern on black craft foam as many times as desired. Cut out the shapes.

2 For each coaster color a small square in the center of the foam using paint pens.

3 Color a purple, blue, magenta, and silver wavy band on each edge of the coaster as shown in the photo, *opposite.* Let the paint dry.

4 Use the gold paint pen to write "ENJOY" or another word over each wavy band. Let dry.

Coaster Pattern

Royal Crowns

Kids will love pretending to be queen or king with these foam crowns.

Glitter
- desired colors

Craft Foam
- 11×17-inch sheets of yellow, white, purple, and red

+ Basic Supplies
- tape measure
- stapler
- tracing paper
- pencil
- scissors
- pinking shears
- paper punch
- hot-glue gun
- glue sticks
- paper plate
- thick white crafts glue

Here's how

1 Use a tape measure to determine your child's head size. The short crown pattern provided on *page 73* is 21 inches in length and the tall crown pattern on *page 72* is 19 inches. If needed staple a second sheet of craft foam on the end to extend the length and to continue the pattern for either crown.

2 Enlarge the patterns on *pages 72–73*. Cut out the shapes. Trace around the shapes on craft foam and cut out.

3 *For the short crown,* cut the edges of the decorative strip with pinking shears and punch holes down the length of the strip as shown in the pattern.

4 *For either crown,* hot-glue the gem shapes to the decorative strips. Hot-glue the finished strip to the bottom of the crown.

5 Roll the crown and staple the overlapping edges together. Apply crafts glue along the edges of the crown points. Working over a paper plate or wastebasket, shake glitter onto the wet glue. For added detail, outline the gems and punched holes with glue; sprinkle on more glitter. Let the glue dry.

continued on page 72

Tall Crown Inner
Layer Pattern

Tall Crown Outer
Layer Pattern

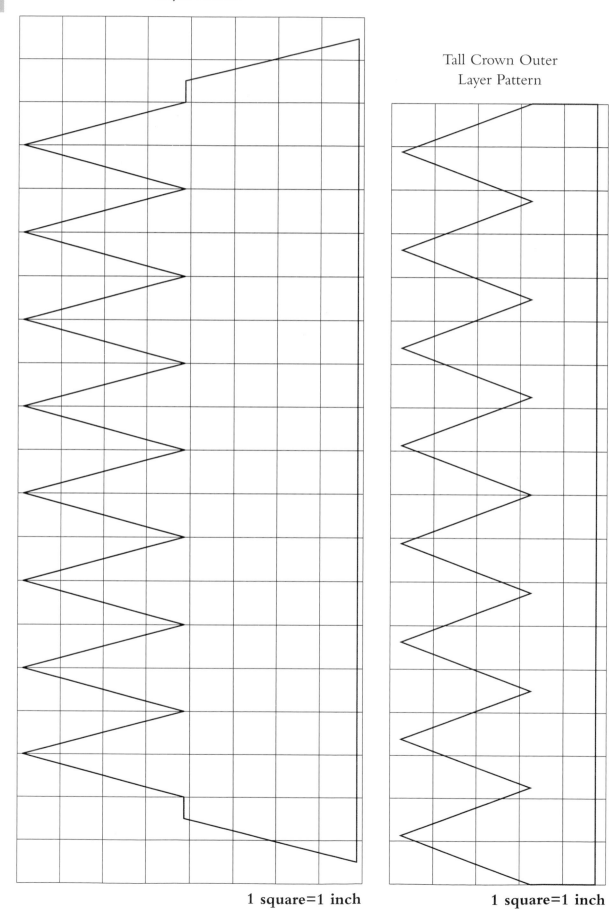

1 square=1 inch

1 square=1 inch

**Tall Crown
Decorative
Strip Pattern**

**Short
Crown
Pattern**

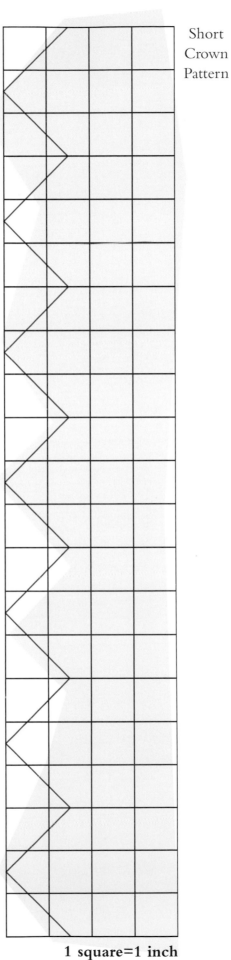

**Short
Crown
Decorative
Strip
Pattern**

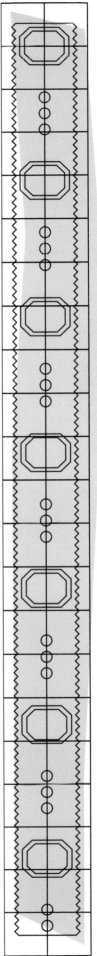

1 square=1 inch

1 square=1 inch

1 square=1 inch

Swishy Fishy Place Mats

Create a playful atmosphere in the kitchen when you set the table with deep-sea characters.

 Acrylic Paints
- black and colors to accent fish

 Craft Foam
- white and desired colors

+ Basic Supplies
- tracing paper
- pencil
- scissors
- thick white crafts glue
- paintbrush

Here's how

1 Enlarge and trace the fish patterns, *opposite.* Cut out the shapes. Trace around the patterns on craft foam. Cut out.

2 Cut out eyes and teeth from contrasting craft foam and glue to fish.

3 Paint pupil in eyes with acrylic paint. *For orange fish* use acrylic paint to add mouth and eyebrows.

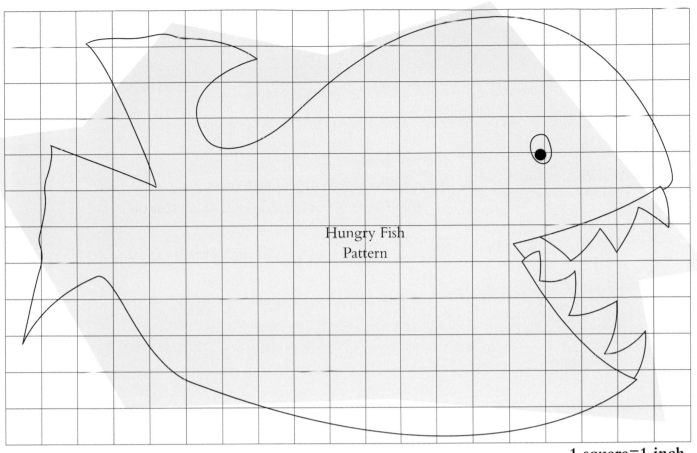

Hungry Fish
Pattern

1 square=1 inch

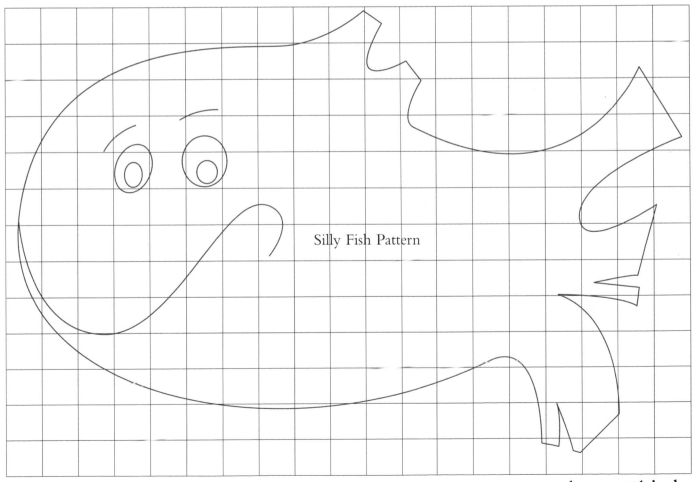

Silly Fish Pattern

1 square=1 inch

Old-World Finials

Wonderful accents, these finials are created from clay that cracks naturally to give vintage appeal.

  Air-Dry Clay
- white

 Acrylic Paints
- cream, burnt umber, and avocado

+ Basic Supplies
- rolling pin
- crafts knife
- toothpick (optional)
- thick white crafts glue
- paintbrush

Here's how

1 Knead the clay to soften. Roll out and flatten clay with a rolling pin.

2 For each base, cut the rolled clay into a small square. For a thicker base, cut one or two more squares the same size and layer them. Continue making square or triangle shapes and stack the pieces. If clay segments don't stack together well, use a toothpick to hold them together while forming the finial. For the top piece, shape a ball, crown, arrow point, or other desired shape. Let the clay dry and harden. Thick shapes may take a few days to harden. The clay may crack naturally as it dries to enhance the old-world appearance.

3 Glue the stacked segments together. Let dry.

4 Paint the finials cream. Let dry. Brush on burnt umber paint and immediately wipe off to create worn tones. Brush on avocado paint and immediately wipe off. Let the paint dry.

Starry-Night Trims

These stars are so easy to make, the kids can share in the fun.

Acrylic Paints
• silver

Craft Foam
• blue

+ Basic Supplies
• tracing paper
• pencil
• scissors
• paintbrush
• wire or cording

Here's how

1 Trace the pattern, *below,* onto tracing paper. Cut out the shape. Trace around pattern on foam, tracing two stars for each ornament.

2 Cut out the stars and make the indicated slits. Paint spirals, spots, dots, or stripes onto both sides of each star. Let the paint dry.

3 Join the stars by threading the slits together. Poke a hole through the top and thread with wire or cording to hang.

Star Ornament
Pattern

Chapter 4

Scrapbook Papers
Ribbons
Rubber Stamps and Pads
Marking Pens

Get out your , look for some brightly colored 🎀, open the 🖃 pad, and find a fresh new set of ✐ to create something FUN!

Holiday Cutout Card

Make a funky holiday card that shares the magic of the season.

Scrapbook Papers
- 2 red prints
- 1 green print

Ribbons
- ⅛-inch-wide black

Rubber Stamp and Pad
- happy holidays stamp
- black pad

+ Basic Supplies
- scissors
- tracing paper
- pencil
- glue stick or double-stick tape

Here's how

1 Enlarge and trace pattern, *below,* and cut out. Place red print papers with wrong sides together and trace pattern on top paper. Cut out both papers. Glue or tape the wrong sides together in all areas except the arch area above the cutout. Score and fold in the sides of the card.

2 Cut out swirls from green paper. Glue swirls on front of card. Glue two swirls together with black ribbon in between them. Repeat this two more times. Insert the ribbons into the arch so the swirls hang into the cutout area. Glue arch closed. Let dry.

3 Stamp green print with "Happy Holidays." Trim a narrow border. Mount on remaining red print; trim to fit in card. Glue message in place.

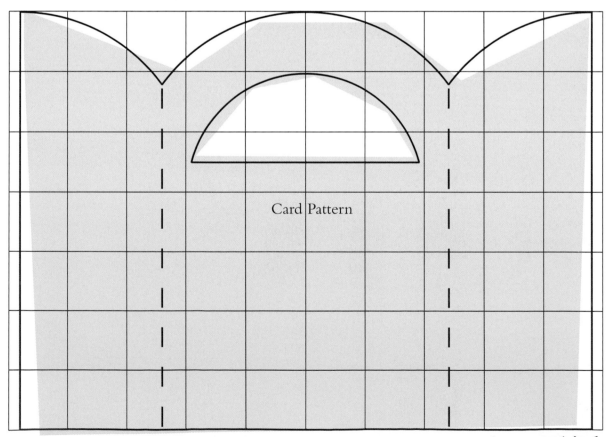

Card Pattern

1 square=1 inch

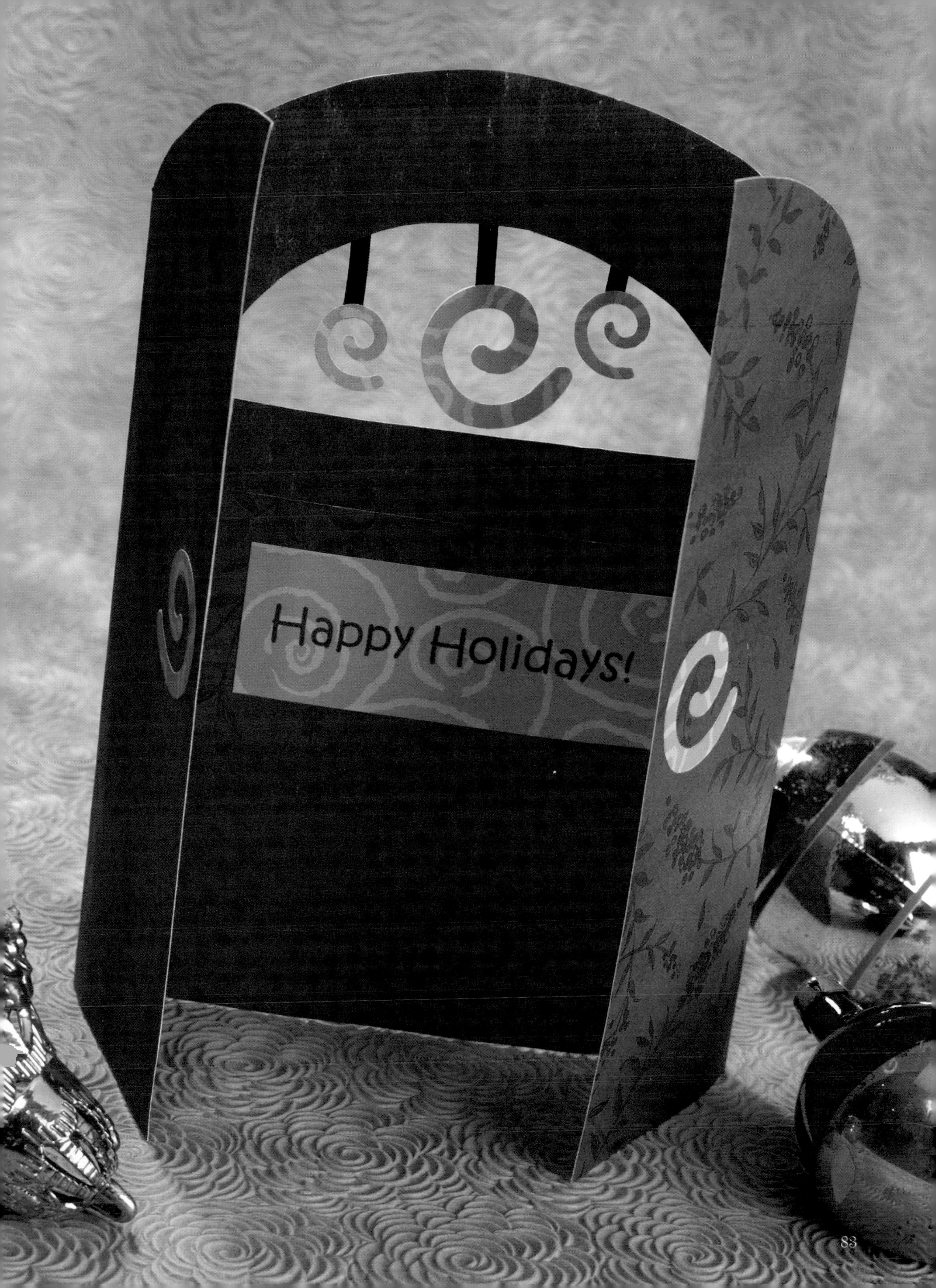
Happy Holidays!

Radiant Angel

Sheer ribbon wings add a glistening touch to this pretty angel shaped from scrapbook papers.

 Scrapbook Papers
- holiday print, ivory, metallic gold, and red
- pink velour paper
- green vellum

 Ribbons
- 16-inch length of wide sheer green with gold wire edge

 Rubber Stamps and Pads
- holly stamp
- metallic gold stamp pad

 Marking Pens
- red

✚ Basic Supplies
- tracing paper
- pencil
- scissors
- crafts knife
- glue stick
- thick white crafts glue

Here's how

1 Trace the patterns, *pages 86–87,* onto tracing paper. Cut out the shapes. Trace around patterns on papers, tracing on fold when necessary. Cut out the dress from the holiday print paper. Cut one star crown from ivory and one from metallic gold. Cut out inner head from pink velour paper. Fringe the edge of the ivory outer head as shown on the pattern. Cut the ruffle and some streamers from red.

2 To make the dress ruffle, score the paper strip as indicated on the pattern, alternating sides. Pleat the scored ruffle.

3 Use the holly stamp and gold ink to stamp the image on green vellum. Color in the berries using a red marking pen. Cut out the holly shapes.

4 Tie the ribbon into a bow. Trim off the ends neatly.

5 Shape the dress piece into a cone. Glue the edges to hold, leaving a ¼-inch opening at top. Use a glue stick to glue ruffle around the bottom edge of the skirt. Glue holly to the top front of the cone.

6 Tightly wrap each red streamer around a pencil. Remove and glue to cone, trailing them from the holly.

7 Glue the bow to the back of the cone using crafts glue.

8 Adhere the ivory star crown on the gold star so that all star points show and are equally spaced. Glue the fringed outer head in the center of the ivory star crown. Glue the pink inner head in the center. Fold one point of the ivory star crown to fit inside cone. Glue to secure.

continued on page 86

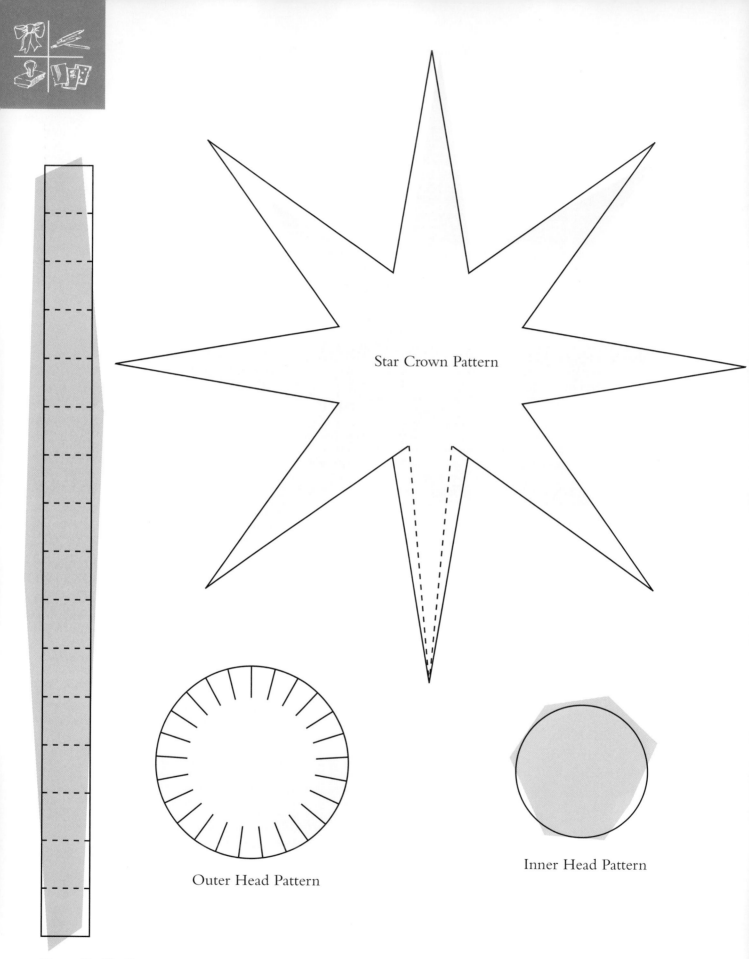

Star Crown Pattern

Outer Head Pattern

Inner Head Pattern

Dress Ruffle Pattern

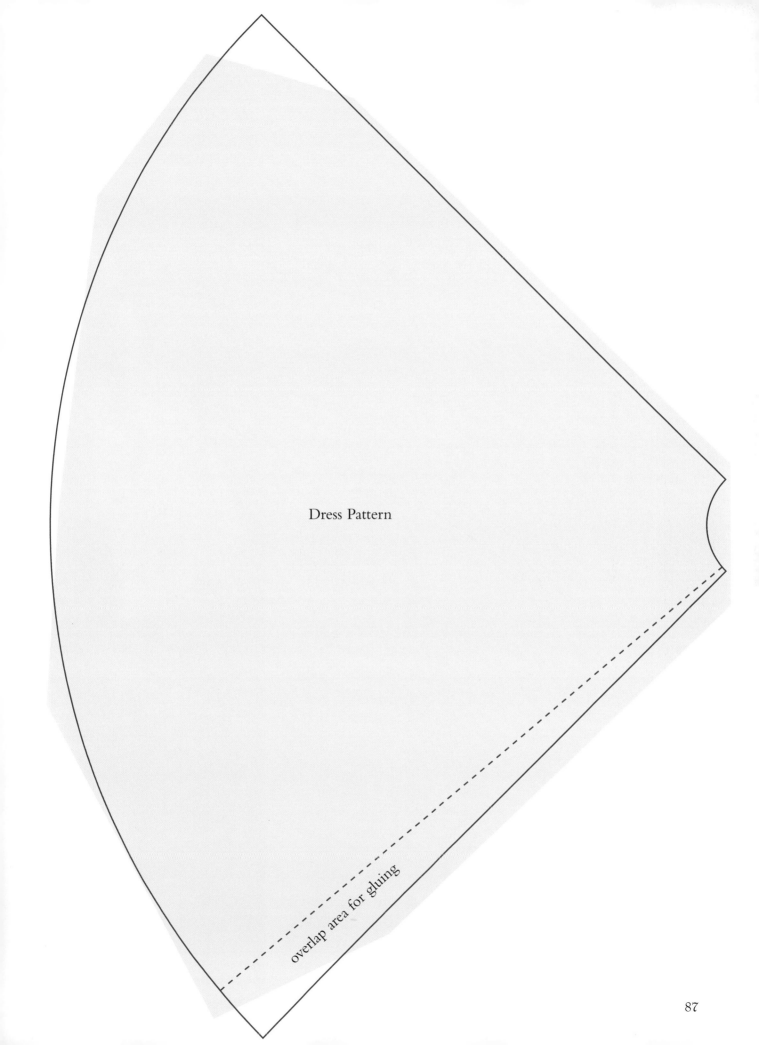

Dress Pattern

overlap area for gluing

Tiny Trees

Make a wonderland of paper trees to decorate your home.

Scrapbook Papers
- assorted green, red, and black

Ribbons
- ⅛-inch-wide black

Rubber Stamps and Pads
- star stamp
- metallic gold stamp pad

Marking Pens
- metallic gold

✚ Basic Supplies
- tracing paper
- pencil
- crafts knife
- double-sided tape or glue stick
- scissors

Here's how

1 Trace the tree pattern, *page 90.* If you wish to make a larger tree, enlarge the pattern on a photocopier to create the tree size you prefer.

2 Cut out the pattern and trace around it on various green scrapbook papers. Using the dotted lines on the pattern as a guide, score and fold the paper shape. Tape or glue the side edges together.

3 To make stars, use a rubber stamp and ink pad or trace the desired patterns, *page 91,* and cut out. Use the patterns to cut shapes from red and black papers. Outline the shapes with gold if desired. Attach the shapes to the trees with glue or tape. Decorate trees with contrasting paper strips. If desired, glue a star to a ribbon and hang from a diamond shape at the treetop. For the multistar topper, knot seven 6-inch lengths of ribbon together. Thread the straight ribbon ends through the point of the tree and glue a star on the end of each ribbon.

continued on page 90

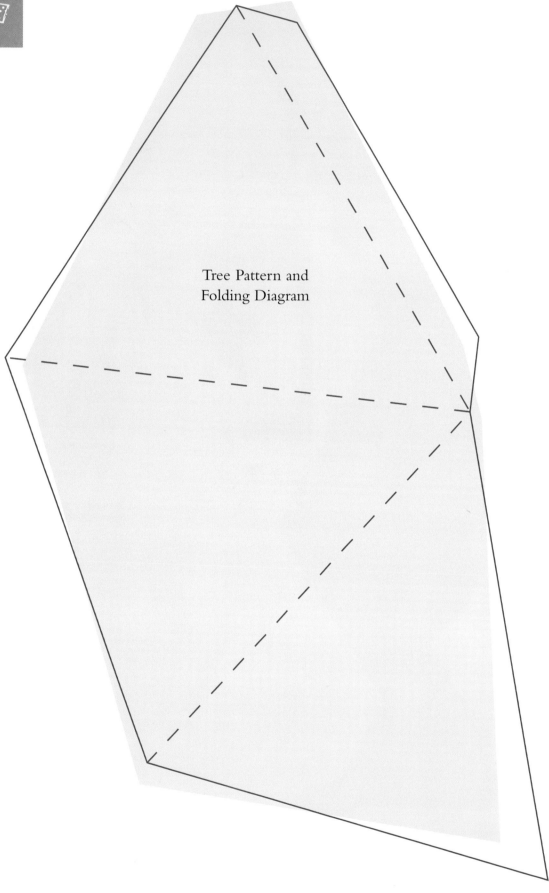

Tree Pattern and
Folding Diagram

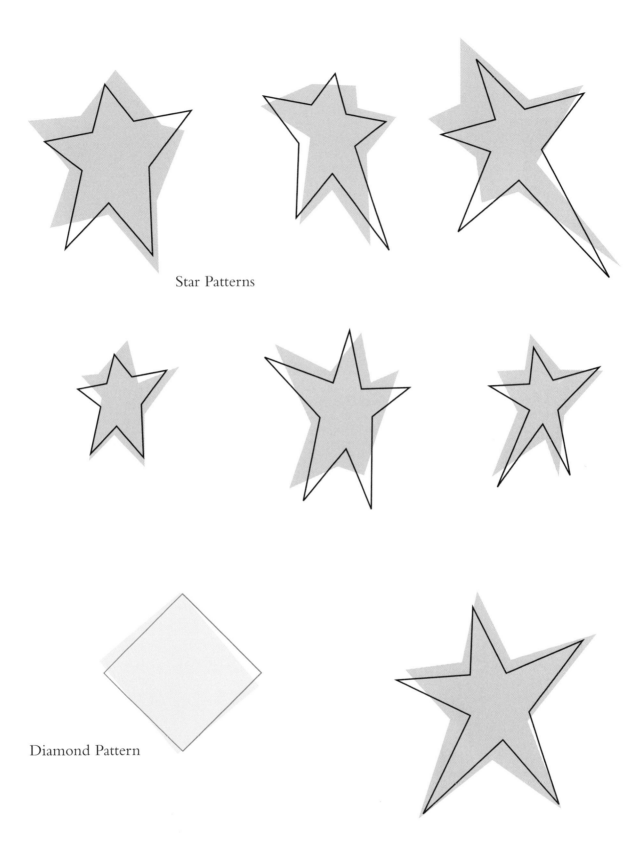

Star Patterns

Diamond Pattern

Holiday Symbols

It's all in the way you fold paper to create fun-to-make ornaments.

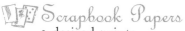
Scrapbook Papers
• desired prints

Ribbons
• silver metallic in ⅛- and ⅜-inch widths

Marking Pens
• silver

+ Basic Supplies
• double-sided tape or glue stick
• paper punch
• scissors
• pencil

Here's how

1 To embellish the scrapbook paper, draw over the designs using a silver marking pen.

2 Enlarge, if needed, and trace the desired ornament pattern, *below* and on *pages 94–95*. Cut out the shapes.

3 For each ornament, fold the paper using the patterns and illustrations, *below* and on *pages 94–95,* as guides. Before securing the ends, attach a ⅜-inch ribbon hanging loop, using the illustration, *page 95,* as a guide for the box-style ornament. For the triangle ornament, thread the hanger through the top. For the pleated ornament, punch two holes opposite each other and thread with ribbon. Tape or glue the ends to secure.

continued on page 94

Pleated Ornament Folding Diagram

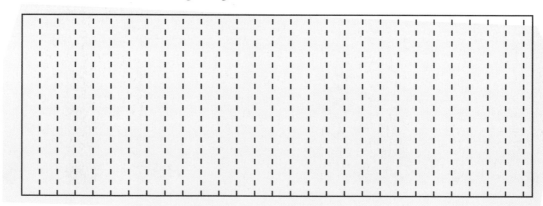

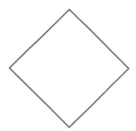

Pleated Ornament
Tassel Pattern
(cut one)

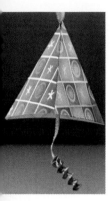

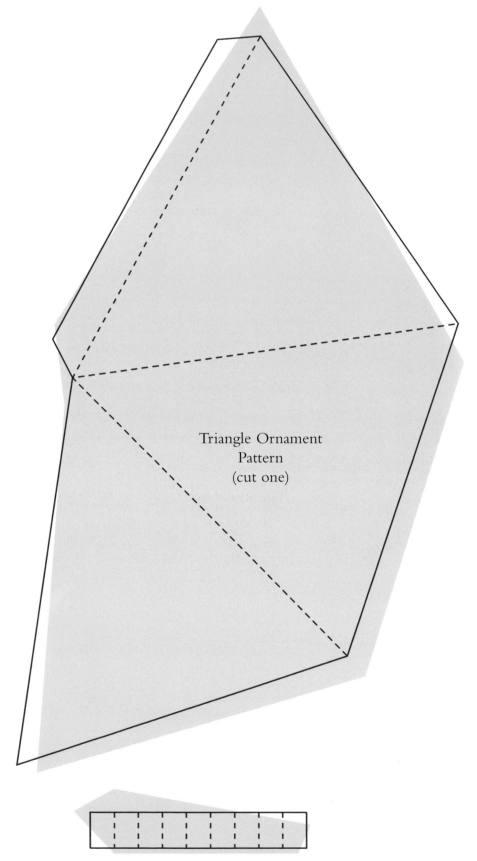

Triangle Ornament
Pattern
(cut one)

Triangle Ornament Tassel Pattern
(cut one)

Box-Style Ornament Folding Diagram

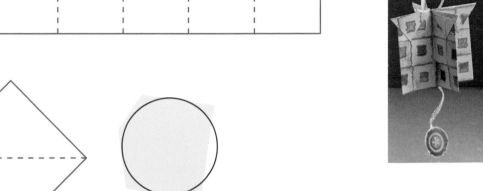

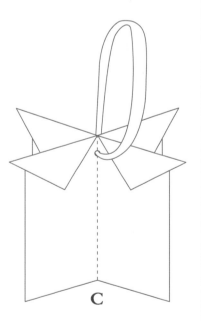

Box-Style Ornament
Topper Pattern (cut four)

Box-Style
Ornament Tassel
Pattern
(cut one)

Box-Style Ornament Diagrams

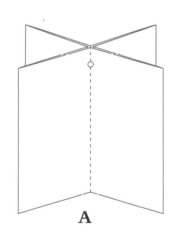

A

Thread ribbon
through the holes
and knot in the
center as shown
in Diagram B.

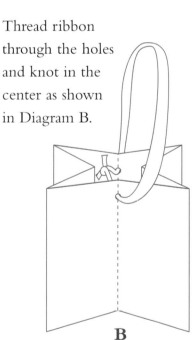

B

Accordion-fold a 2½×11-inch
strip as shown in Diagram A,
above. With two flaps on each
side, punch a hole ½ inch from
the top. Glue down the
overlapping flap.

C

Fold paper squares in half,
point to point, and glue to
the top of each flap as
shown in Diagram C.

Gift Box Greetings

A birthday is meant for surprises, and this card captures the anticipation.

Scrapbook Papers
- solid lime green and purple plaid

Ribbons
- ¼-inch-wide turquoise checked

Marking Pens
- purple

+ Basic Supplies
- ruler
- pencil
- scissors
- glue stick
- crafts knife

Here's how

1 Cut lime green paper to measure 8½×6½ inches. With the short ends together, fold the paper in half.

2 Cut a 4×6¼-inch piece of plaid paper. Use a pencil and ruler to measure in ⅜ inch and mark as the inside border. Cut along the markings to make a frame. Cut a 1⅝×2¼-inch rectangle for the package. Draw swirly designs on the package using a marking pen.

3 Glue the plaid border centered on the front of the card. Glue the package ¾ inch up from the bottom of the frame, centering left to right.

4 Using a crafts knife cut ¼-inch-long horizontal slits in the green paper at the center of the package top and bottom. Cut a 10-inch-long piece of ribbon. Thread the ribbon through the slits, bringing the tails to the right side. Tie a small bow at the package top. Trim the ribbon ends.

5 Write "it's your day!" with a marking pen.

Stamped Salutations

The popular art of rubber stamping makes kids' play out of this classy card.

Here's how

1 Cut the black paper to measure 5×8 inches. Measure to find the center fold line. To score the card, lay ruler along fold line and lightly run knife along edge of ruler without cutting through the paper. Fold along score line.

2 Trim a piece of colored paper to fit front panel. To leave the blank space for words in the middle of the card, lay a piece of paper on the area. Stamp the design and remove the paper.

3 Write "Happy Birthday!" with black marking pen.

4 Use a black marking pen to draw a curvy edge to separate the stamping from the "Happy Birthday!" Glue stamped paper onto black card. Tie a green ribbon around the folded edge.

 Scrapbook Papers
- black glossy
- colored

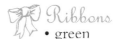 Ribbons
- green

 Rubber Stamps and Pads
- leaf stamp
- black ink pad

 Marking Pens
- black

+ Basic Supplies
- ruler
- scissors
- crafts knife
- glue stick

Embroidered Stationery

A few simple stitches of silk ribbon create charming notes.

Scrapbook Papers
• solid color

Ribbons
• 4 mm or 7 mm silk in desired colors

✛ Basic Supplies
• scissors
• tracing paper
• pencil
• darning needle
• glue (optional)

Here's how

1 Cut the scrapbook paper to the desired size for card; fold in half.

2 Trace the desired design, *below,* onto tracing paper. Unfold the card and place it on a protected work surface. Place the tracing on the note card front.

3 Use a darning needle to pierce the design into the paper pattern and note card. Using the pattern holes and diagrams as guides, stitch the design with silk ribbon. Knot the ends on the back of the card.

4 Decorate the note card and envelope with running stitches or flat pieces of ribbon glued in place.

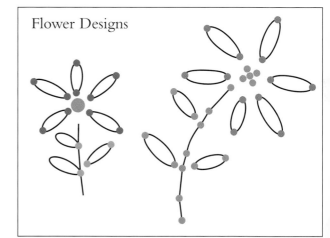

Flower Designs

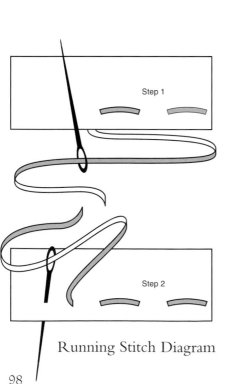

Running Stitch Diagram

Straight Stitch Diagram

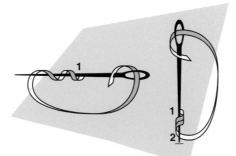

French Knot Diagram

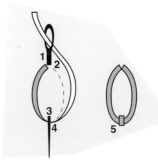

Lazy Daisy Stitch Diagram

Time-for-a-Party Hat

Choose festive scrapbook papers to make these full-of-fun party hats.

Scrapbook Papers
- desired colors and prints

Ribbons
- 1-inch-wide

+ Basic Supplies
- tracing paper
- pencil
- scissors
- thick white crafts glue
- ruler
- paper punch

Here's how

1 Trace and cut out patterns, *opposite*. To make the hat pattern, fold a 12-inch square in half and align the fold with the fold line on pattern. Trace around shapes on scrapbook papers; cut out. Apply glue to hat flap, roll paper into a cone, and glue edges together.

2 *For the curled-brim hat,* cut out five large triangles in contrasting paper and glue to another print, wrong sides together. Cut out. Roll top edge forward. Glue triangles around base of hat. Glue a ½-inch-wide strip around bottom edge of hat. Curl small triangles.

3 Cut out five small triangles and glue to base, positioning them between the larger triangles. Cut seven 1⅛-inch-diameter circles and glue one to the tip of each curled triangle and two to hat tip.

4 Punch a hole on each side of the hat. Thread an 18-inch length of ribbon through each hole; knot on inside.

5 *For the fringe-brim hat,* use the bottom edge of hat for a pattern and cut two 2-inch strips from different papers. Glue these two strips together with a thin line of glue down the center back of one strip. Allow to dry. Cut narrow slits for fringe on both of the long edges leaving a ½-inch solid area in the center of the strip. Glue the fringe around bottom of hat.

6 Cut a 4×2-inch strip of paper. Fringe on one long side, stopping ½ inch from bottom. Roll this strip around a pencil and glue overlap. Slip bottom of fringed tube over tip of hat and glue. Repeat Step 4 to complete.

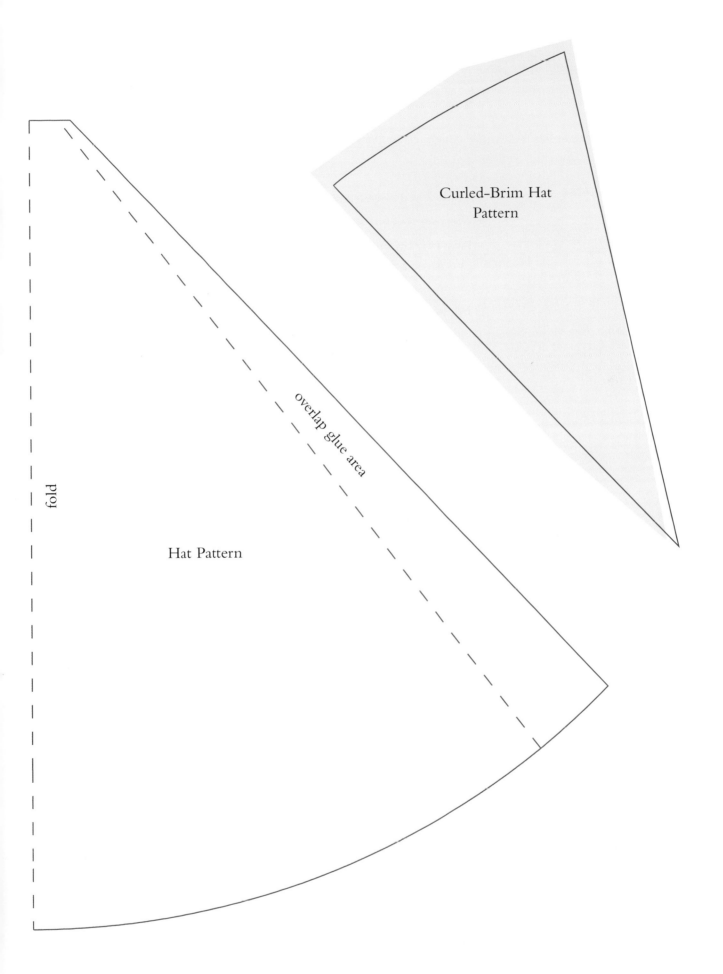

Curled–Brim Hat
Pattern

fold

overlap glue area

Hat Pattern

Spinning Stars

Fill your holiday tree with clever stars in every color of the galaxy.

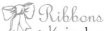 Scrapbook Papers
- desired print

 Ribbons
- ⅛-inch-wide ribbon

+ Basic Supplies
- tracing paper
- pencil
- scissors
- double-stick tape or glue stick
- paper punch

Here's how

1 Trace the patterns, *below,* and cut out. Fold paper right sides together; trace ornament pattern twice. Cut out shapes and tape or glue the wrong sides together. Cut a slit in the top of one shape and at the bottom of the other. Fit together.

2 Punch holes in each top and bottom point of ornament. Slightly fold each ornament piece lengthwise and punch a hole halfway down the fold. Thread pieces of ribbon through the bottom holes; knot. Thread ribbon through the top holes, leaving a loop for hanging; knot and cut off excess.

3 Trace around the small rectangle pattern four times. Cut out and punch holes on each side of the rectangle. Begin threading ribbon through a center hole and then thread ribbon through both holes of one rectangle per quadrant of the ornament. Knot ribbon and cut off excess.

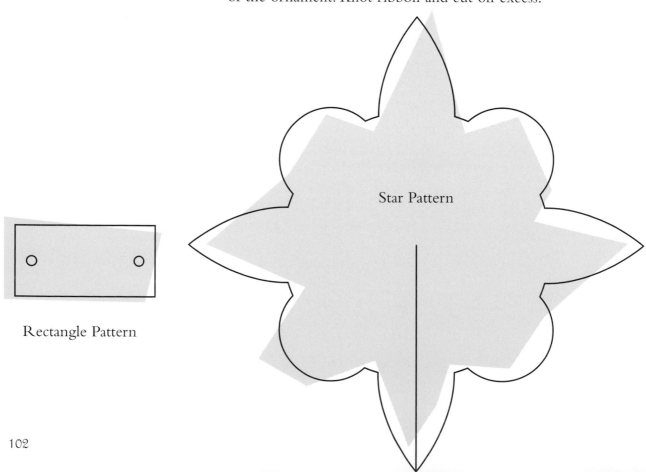

Star Pattern

Rectangle Pattern

Handsome Greetings

Surprise someone special with this stylish, richly colored card.

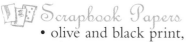

Scrapbook Papers
- olive and black print, olive, and black

Ribbons
- ¼-inch black

Rubber Stamps and Pad
- fleur-de-lis stamp
- black ink pad

+ Basic Supplies
- scissors
- crafts knife
- double-sided tape or glue stick
- ruler; pencil

Here's how

1 Cut print paper and olive paper to 7×10 inches. Score and fold in half. Cut a 1¼-inch square from black paper.

2 Stamp image on coordinating paper. Cut image out in a 1-inch square. Tape to black square. Center and tape square to card 2½ inches from top of print-paper card.

3 Measure 1½ inches from top of card. Cut ¼-inch-long slits every ½ inch. Thread black ribbon through the slits and tie in a bow on the side. Tape olive paper in the card as a liner. To embellish the liner, cut two strips of scrapbook paper ½×7 inches and tape where desired.

All-My-Heart Card

Vellum paper and pretty ribbons make this card an elegant greeting.

Here's how

1 Cut teal paper to 7×10 inches, score, and fold. Cut light teal paper to same dimension, score, and fold. Cut vellum to 4×5½ inches.

2 Stamp leftover paper with silver hearts and cut to approximately 1¼×4 inches. Use double-sided tape to adhere teal ribbon to upper and lower edges of front of card. Wrap one edge around right edge of card and make a small slit on left edge back of card to insert and tape down.

3 Center the vellum on card. At the top center of the vellum, cut a slit through both layers. Cut a slit at the top of the heart-stamped card stock.

4 Layer the papers on the card front. Cut a 2-inch piece of ribbon. Insert the ends into each of the slits, leaving a loop. Insert a bow through the loop. Pull the ends of loop tight and tape to inside of card. Tape the light teal paper inside the card as a liner.

 Scrapbook Papers
- teal and light teal
- silver heart-print vellum

 Ribbons
- ⅜-inch silver; ⅛-inch teal

Rubber Stamps
and Pads
- heart stamp
- silver ink pad

+ Basic Supplies
- scissors
- crafts knife
- ruler; pencil
- double-sided tape or glue stick

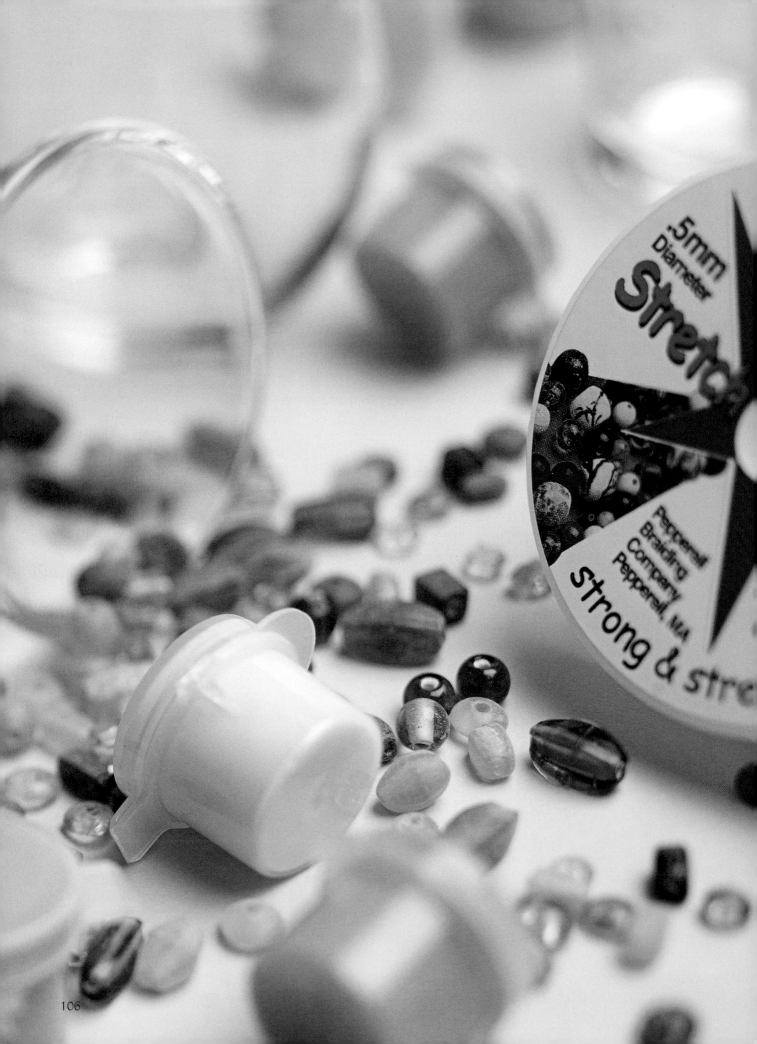

Chapter 5

Glass Votive Candleholders

Glass Paints

Beads

Elastic Cord

Choose a pretty 🔲, and some ✏️ for color, tiny 🫘 for sparkle, 〰️ with plenty of stretch, and you can make any craft project in this chapter!

Floral Candleholders

Candleholders in subtle colors provide pretty pastel backgrounds for these easy-to-paint floral designs.

Glass Votive Candleholders
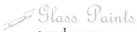
- square pastel or clear

Glass Paints
- red, maroon, pink, white, green, purple, blue, and yellow

+ Basic Supplies
- pencil
- artist's paintbrushes

Here's how

1 *For all votive candleholders,* wash and dry the candleholder. Avoid touching the areas to be painted.

2 *For the red flowers,* dip a pencil eraser in red paint and dot once on the top half of the candleholder as shown in Photo A, *below.* Let dry. Dip a paintbrush handle in maroon and add three dots at the top of each flower as shown in Photo B. Add five pink dots in the same manner. Dip a pencil tip in white to highlight each flower. Paint green leaves and stems. Let dry.

3 *For the purple flowers,* mix purple with white until the desired color is achieved. Dip a pencil eraser in the paint and dot randomly on the top half of the candleholder. Let dry. Dip a pencil tip in purple paint to add three dots at the bottom of each flower. Apply one white dot at the top of each flower. Paint green leaves and stems. Let dry.

4 *For the blue flowers,* dip the paintbrush handle into blue paint. Randomly dot the paint in flower shapes on the candleholder. Let dry. Dip a pencil eraser in yellow and dot in the center of each flower. Dip pencil tip in white to highlight each petal. Paint green leaves and stems. Let dry.

5 Bake candleholder in oven if directed by paint manufacturer.

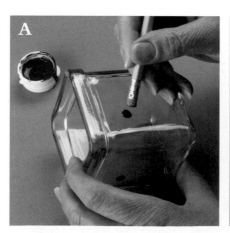
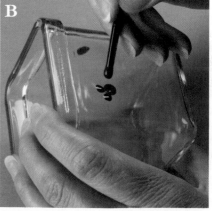

Bead-azzled Cups

Glass beads transform simple votive candleholders into containers that sparkle with holiday light.

 Glass Votive Candleholders
- desired shape

 Beads
- assorted tube and round

+ Basic Supplies
- pencil
- strong glue, such as E6000
- tweezers

Here's how

1 Wash and dry the candleholder. Use a pencil to sketch a simple design around the glass.

2 Dip beads into glue and glue onto the lines using tweezers to place the beads.

3 Add a ring of beads around the rim of the votive if desired. Let the glue dry.

Leaf-Laden Duo

Connect two votive holders side by side for double the candlelight.

Here's how

1 Place two straight-sided votive candleholders side by side.

2 Using gold elastic cord, tie the votive holders together with a figure eight wrap. Repeat this twice, tying ends of cord together in a knot between the two candleholders.

3 Hook leaf-shape glass beads over the cord.

 Glass Votive
Candleholders
- 2 with straight sides

 Beads
- leaf-shape glass on wire hooks

Elastic Cord
- gold

+ Basic Supplies
- scissors

Little Love Light

Float romantic candlelight on a sea of love with this fringed and gilded candleholder.

Glass Votive Candleholders
- clear cylinder

Beads
- red fringe

**Glass Paints**
- metallic red and gold paint pens

+ **Basic Supplies**
- pencil; tracing paper
- scissors; tape
- glue, such as Goop
- paint-brush
- heart-shape floating candle

Here's how

1 Wash and dry the candleholder. Avoid touching the areas to be painted.

2 Draw a scroll pattern on a strip of tracing paper. Tape the pattern inside the candleholder near the bottom.

3 Paint the design on the outside of the candleholder. Remove the pattern. Let dry. Glue fringe around the top of the candleholder. Fill the candleholder about one-third full with water; lower in a heart-shape candle.

Make a Wish!

Make someone's birthday extra special with this festive birthday candleholder.

Here's how

1 Wash and dry the candleholder. Avoid touching the areas to be painted.

2 Paint stripes of a variety of colors and heights around the candleholder. Paint flames. Let dry. Accent the candle shapes with a thin line of black paint. Let the paint dry.

3 Bake the painted candleholder in the oven according to the paint manufacturer's directions. Let cool. Fill with sand and position candles in the sand.

Glass Votive Candleholder
• clear glass

Glass Paints
• desired colors

+ Basic Supplies
• paintbrush
• birthday candles
• sand

Pastel Paisley Holder

Pretty colors and graceful brushstrokes give this clear glass votive holder a look of elegance.

 Glass Votive Candleholders
- clear with flat sides

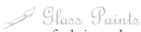 Glass Paints
- fuchsia, teal, royal blue, and white

+ Basic Supplies
- disposable plate
- small round paintbrush

Here's how

1 Wash and dry the votive holder. Avoid touching the areas to be painted.

2 Place a small amount of each paint color on the plate. Using fuchsia and royal blue, paint a paisley design approximately half the size of a golf ball, in the center of one side of the votive holder. Blend the colors.

3 Highlight just inside the paisley using a blend of white and fuchsia.

4 For the designs around the paisley, make groups of brushstrokes in all of the paint colors. Vary the size and direction of the strokes as shown in the photo, *opposite.*

5 To create dots to border the paisley and in the background, dip the paintbrush handle in paint and dot onto the surface.

6 When the paint used on the paisley is dry, add brushstrokes of white and of a royal blue-teal mixture. Let the paint dry.

7 Bake the painted votive holder in the oven according to the paint manufacturer's instructions. Let cool.

Beaded Wrist Wraps

In minutes you can create a designer-style bracelet to wear with pride.

 Beads
- assorted colored and metallic glass

 Elastic Cord
- 1.5 mm clear

 Basic Supplies
- scissors
- ruler

Here's how

1 Cut a 10-inch piece of elastic for the single-strand bracelet styles and three 10-inch pieces for the triple-strand style.

2 *For the single-strand bracelets,* string beads on elastic in the desired order. Wrap the beaded elastic around wrist to check fit; knot the elastic ends together. Thread the elastic ends back through several beads. Cut excess elastic.

3 *For the triple-strand bracelet,* use approximately 6 large beads and 54 small beads. Knot the three elastic strands together at one end to keep beads from slipping off. Thread all three elastic pieces through a big bead. Thread three small beads on each piece of elastic and then slip the three ends through another large bead. Continue beading in this pattern until the desired length is achieved. Knot the elastic ends together. Thread the elastic ends back through several beads. Cut excess elastic.

Western Glow

Blended bands of paint and white seed beads coat a clear glass votive holder with the look of the southwest.

Glass Votive Candleholders
- round clear

Glass Paints
- black, red, turquoise, and royal

Beads
- white seed

Basic Supplies
- small paintbrush
- strong crafts glue, such as E6000
- toothpick

Here's how

1 Wash and dry the votive holder. Avoid touching the areas to be painted.

2 Paint the top half of the votive candleholder black, feathering the bottom edge as shown in Photo A, *below.*

3 While the black paint is wet, blend in a ¼-inch-wide stripe of red at the bottom of the black, leaving a border of black as shown in Photo B. Continue blending in ¼-inch bands of turquoise and royal. Let the paint dry.

4 Paint the rim with glue and dip in beads. Let dry.

5 Glue a zigzag of beads at the bottom of the feathered black area, using a toothpick to place the beads on dots of glue, as shown in Photo C. Let dry.

A

B

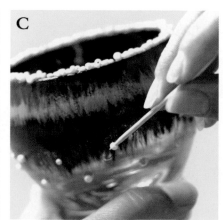

C

Simply Beaded

Great for an impromptu dinner or a last-minute gift, these fun candleholders are a snap to make.

 Glass Votive Candleholder
- clear glass

 Beads
- glass and seed in desired colors

 Elastic Cord
- clear

✚ Basic Supplies
- scissors

Here's how

1 Wrap the elastic loosely around the votive as many times as you wish for the beaded design. Cut off the elastic.

2 String beads on the elastic in the desired arrangement. *To make a bracelet with the round layered beads,* thread the cord through the back of a flat bead, then a small bead, and thread the cord back through flat bead. Knot cord ends.

3 Place the beaded rings around the votive.

Stars on Stripes

Use colored elastic to create bands that sparkle on a star-studded candleholder.

Here's how

1 String flat metallic star beads on red elastic cord.

2 Tie elastic tightly around a glass votive candleholder. Knot cord ends. Apply a dot of glue to knot and let dry.

3 Cut off excess cord. Repeat for two more rows.

Glass Votive Candleholder
• frosted flowerpot shape

Elastic Cord
• red

Beads
• flat metallic stars

+ Basic Supplies
• thick white crafts glue
• scissors

A Coat of Beads

Glass beads transform simple votive candleholders into containers that shimmer with light.

Glass Votive Candleholder
- clear, desired shape

Beads
- assorted seed

+ Basic Supplies
- thick white crafts glue
- 2 disposable plates
- small sponge paintbrush
- tea light

Here's how

1 Squeeze glue onto a plate. Using a slightly damp sponge brush, apply a generous coat of glue over a small section of the votive candleholder without covering the bottom.

2 Hold the votive candleholder over a second plate and sprinkle glass beads over the glue area. Press the beads into the glue with your fingers.

3 Shake the excess beads back into the container. Continue gluing and sprinkling beads to completely cover the holder. Let the glue dry. Set a tea light in the holder.

Easy-Does-It

In minutes you can personalize glass votive holders with a ring of beads or painted fingerprints.

Here's how

1 Wash and dry the votive cup. *Avoid touching the areas to be painted. For the fingerprint votive,* use finger to dab paint around the candleholder. Let dry. Bake the candleholder in the oven if instructed by the paint manufacturer.

2 *For the beaded votive,* thread desired beads on elastic cord. Tie the cord around the top of the candleholder. Trim the excess cord.

Glass Votive Candleholders
• clear, with ridge at top for beaded style

Glass Paints
• iridescent in desired colors

Beads
• assorted

Elastic Cord
• clear

+ Basic Supplies
• scissors

Confetti Cups

Dots of paint lend the look of confetti on this playful votive holder.

 Glass Votive
Candleholders
- frosted votive

 Glass Paints
- blue, yellow, white, green, purple, red, turquoise, and pink

 Beads
- small glass tubes and crimp beads

 Elastic Cord
- clear

 Basic Supplies
- small paintbrush
- crimping tool
- scissors
- thick white crafts glue (optional)

Here's how

1 Wash and dry the votive cup. Avoid touching the areas to be painted.

2 To make dots on the votive, dip a paintbrush handle in glass paint and dot onto the surface. Wash and dry the handle each time a new color is used. Let the paint dry. Bake the candleholder in the oven if instructed by the paint manufacturer.

3 String tube and crimp beads on the elastic. At the end, thread both cord ends through a crimp bead and squeeze crimp bead to secure the elastic and beads. Cut off excess elastic. Wrap the string of beads around the votive cup where desired, using glue to secure if needed. Let dry.

Honeycomb Hues

Band the ridges in beehive-style holders with small beaded bracelets in all your favorite colors.

 Glass Votive Candleholder
- honeycomb-style

 Beads
- assorted glass

 Elastic Cord
- clear

 Basic Supplies
- scissors

Here's how

1 For each votive holder bracelet, cut a piece of elastic cord 3 inches longer than the desired bracelet length.

2 Thread beads onto cord, occasionally checking the fit around the votive holder.

3 Knot the ends and tuck each cord end back through several beads; trim off the excess cord.

4 Position the bracelets on the desired votive ridges.

Last-Minute Lighting

In minutes you can add a sophisticated touch to a clear glass votive holder.

Here's how

1 String 8 to 12 gold pony beads on a piece of black elastic.

2 Tie the elastic around the sides of a large square votive candleholder. Position the beads in a pleasing arrangement. Repeat the bead stringing for one or two more lengths of elastic.

3 Add a dot of glue to the knots and hide each knot inside a bead.

Glass Votive
Candleholder
• clear square

Elastic Cord
• black

Beads
• gold pony

+ Basic Supplies
• thick white crafts glue

Primarily Primary

Green joins up with the primary colors to give the ridges of a votive holder a lively finish.

 **Glass Votive Candleholder**
- clear glass with vertical ridges

 **Beads**
- blue tube

 **Glass Paints**
- green, red, yellow, and blue

+ Basic Supplies
- paintbrush
- thick white crafts glue

Here's how

1 Wash and dry the votive cup. Avoid touching the areas to be painted.

2 To paint ridges of votive, paint part of a ridge with one color and blend into another if desired. Alternate the colors so the votive has a uniform look. Let the paint dry.

3 Glue tube beads randomly along edge of ridges. Let dry.

Rainbow Rims

Dab paints and allow them to blend into one another for a color-drenched border.

Here's how

1 Wash and dry the votive holder. Avoid touching the areas to be painted.

2 To paint the rim of the votive holder, start with one color of paint and dab small blotches of color around the rim. Rinse out the paintbrush. Continue dabbing colors around the rim, allowing the colors to bleed into one another. When the rim is completely covered with paint, let it dry.

3 Bake the votive holder in the oven according to the paint manufacturer's directions. Let the votive holder cool.

Glass Votive Candleholders
- clear flowerpot shape

Glass Paints
- purple, blue, yellow, green, and magenta

+ Basic Supplies
- paintbrush

Chapter 6

🪴 Clay Flowerpots

🧱 Polymer Clay

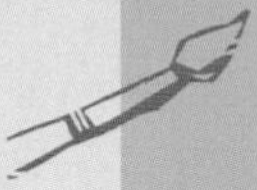

🖌 Acrylic Paints

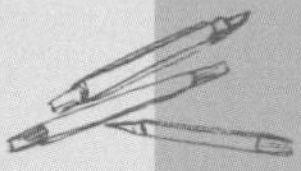

🖊 Marking Pens

Pick out a variety of 🪴, soften up your favorite colors of 🧱, get a palette full of 🖌, and break out some brand-new 🖊 to make something creative!

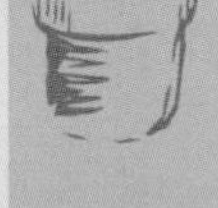

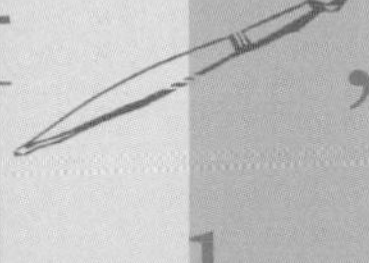

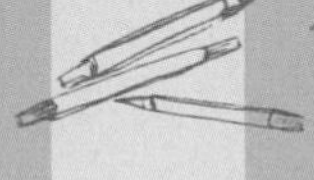

Artfully Handled Vase

Striking colors and simple lines make this clay-embellished flowerpot a work of art.

 Clay Flowerpots
- 8-inch high terra-cotta

 Polymer Clay
- 2 desired colors

 Acrylic Paints
- 2 desired colors

 Basic Supplies
- paintbrush
- glass baking dish
- fork

Here's how

1 Paint the pot base and brim the desired colors. Let the paint dry.

2 Use half a square of clay for the handles. Divide the clay piece in half and form two ropes the same length and diameter.

3 Shape the ropes to form a handle for each side of the flowerpot, curving in spiral shapes as shown in the photo, *opposite*, and the diagram, *below*. Press the shapes against the flowerpot.

4 Form small balls from a contrasting clay. Press at the base of the flowerpot and on each clay handle. To add texture to any clay pieces, press with the tines of a fork.

5 Bake the clay-embellished flowerpot in the oven according to the clay manufacturer's instructions, not exceeding 235° F. Let cool.

Handle Diagram

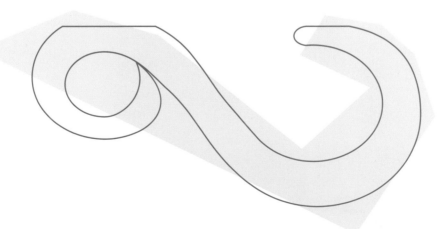

All Abuzz

Simple painted motifs and marking pen accents bring a playful touch to these stacked flowerpots.

 Clay Flowerpots
- 2 terra-cotta flowerpots with saucers

 Acrylic Paints
- yellow, white, and black

 Marking Pens
- black permanent

+ Basic Supplies
- ruler
- pencil
- paintbrush
- strong glue, such as E6000

Here's how

1 Using a ruler and pencil, mark off evenly spaced vertical lines below the rims of the flowerpots. Paint the stripes, alternating with white and yellow. Paint the saucers yellow and their rims black.

2 Paint one flowerpot brim yellow and the other black. Let the paint dry. Paint contrasting diamond shapes around each rim and let dry. Dot white paint where diamonds meet.

3 Invert a flowerpot and glue to an inverted saucer. Glue another flowerpot to the upside-down pot, positioning so the yellow stripes lead into white stripes. Glue the remaining saucer on the top. Let the glue dry.

4 Referring to the patterns, *below,* draw two or three bees buzzing around the flowerpot candleholder with black marking pen.

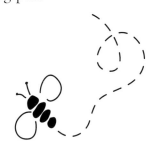

Bee Patterns

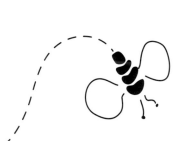

Millefiori Pots

Create and slice clay coils to trim a flowerpot brim with striking patterns.

 Clay Flowerpots
- 2½- and 4-inch-high terra-cotta

 Polymer Clay
- tan, white, pink, lavender, and purple or tan, white, and light and dark blue

 Basic Supplies
- rolling pin
- crafts knife
- glass baking dish

Millefiori assembly ideas

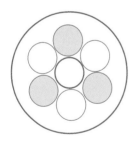

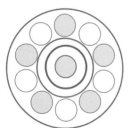

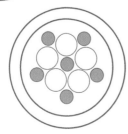

Here's how

1 Knead the clay to make it pliable. To make the design "canes," roll pea-size balls of clay into long thin coils. Use the diagrams, *below left,* for ideas. Select one of the coils to be the center of the cane. Stack contrasting-colored coils around the center cane. To make a larger cane continue adding layers of different-color coils until the desired thickness is reached. Create canes that range from ¼ to ½ inch in diameter.

2 Use a rolling pin to flatten a section of plain colored clay into a very thin sheet. Wrap it around a cane to make a solid border.

3 Use a crafts knife to carefully cut away any overlapping clay. Gently roll the wrapped cane to compress the inner stacks. Set the canes aside.

4 Roll a solid-color clay section until it is ¼ inch thick. Wrap the flattened clay around the rim of the flowerpot; smooth the edges. Make small slits along the rim of the clay to prevent it from cracking in the oven. Slice slivers off the canes and press them randomly onto the clay-covered rim. Bake according to manufacturer's directions.

Floral Photo Pot

Plant clay flowers in a terra-cotta pot for a beautiful way to display favorite photographs.

 Clay Flowerpot
- small- and medium-size terra-cotta with saucer

 Polymer Clay
- bright pink, burgundy, blue, yellow, purple, and green

 Acrylic Paint
- green

 Markers
- dark green

+ Basic Supplies
- rolling pin
- decorative-edge scissors
- cardboard
- thick white crafts glue

Here's how

1 Paint the flowerpots and saucers green. Let the paint dry. Using the marking pen, stripe the edges of the saucer and the rims of the flowerpots.

2 Use one-half square of bright pink clay and roll until flat. Use decorative-edge scissors to cut the clay into a square. Drape the clay square over the inverted saucer.

3 Shape leaves and flowers from clay. To make flowers, roll various-size round circles and press together or make several small balls as petals and roll contrasting balls for the center. For the roses, roll clay flat and cut into strips. Roll strips to shape a rose.

4 Place leaves around the rim of the small flowerpot. Arrange the flowers in the pot as desired. Press the edge of the cardboard into the top of the flowers to allow space to hold a photo.

5 Press two clay flowers and leaves on the rim of the inverted medium-size flowerpot.

6 Place the clay embellished flowerpots and saucer in the oven and bake according to the clay manufacturer's instructions, not exceeding 235°F. Let cool. Glue the components together. Glue any loosened pieces in place. Let the glue dry.

Utilitarian Kitchen Caddy

Bold clay shapes blanket a terra-cotta flowerpot for a cleverly disguised kitchen utensil container.

Clay Flowerpots
- 8-inch-high terra-cotta flowerpot

Polymer Clay
- red, orange, ocher, white, black, and green

✛ Basic Supplies
- rolling pin
- straight and decorative-edge scissors
- knife, pencil, bottle cap, or other item to make impression
- thick white crafts glue (optional)
- glass baking dish

Here's how

1 On a smooth, flat work surface, roll out each clay color separately until approximately ⅛ inch thick. Cut irregular or square shapes from the flattened clay pieces and press onto the flowerpot.

2 For details, roll out pieces of clay and cut strips with straight and decorative-edge scissors as shown in Photo A, *below*. Place on base clay.

3 Use a knife, pencil point, eraser end, or objects such as a bottle cap to make impressions as shown in Photo B.

4 To make a twisted clay rope, roll out two different colors of clay into long smooth lengths about ¼ inch thick. Hold together on one end and twist from the other, twisting evenly and slowly as shown in Photo C. The rope will become thinner the more it is twisted. Press ropes on pot.

5 For dots, roll clay into round balls and press onto clay.

6 After the flowerpot is covered with clay, bake it according to the clay manufacturer's instructions. Let cool. If needed, glue loosened clay pieces to the flowerpot.

A

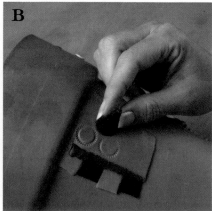

B

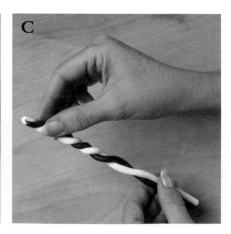

C

Artistic Flowerpot

Transform an ordinary terra-cotta pot into a wildly vivid work of art!

 Clay Flowerpots
- desired size

 Polymer Clay
- red, orange, yellow, white, black, green, light blue, purple, and royal

 **Basic Supplies**
- rolling pin
- straight and decorative-edge scissors
- knife, pencil, bottle cap, or other item to make impression
- thick white crafts glue (optional)
- glass baking dish

Here's how

1 On a smooth, flat work surface, roll out each clay color separately until approximately ⅛ inch thick. Cut straight-edge shapes from the flattened clay pieces and press onto the flowerpot.

2 For details, roll out pieces of clay and cut strips with straight and decorative-edge scissors as shown in Photo A, *page 140.* Place on base clay.

3 Use a knife, pencil point, eraser end, or objects such as a bottle cap to make impressions as shown in Photo B, *page 140.*

4 To make a twisted clay rope, roll out two different colors of clay into long smooth lengths about ¼ inch thick. Hold together on one end and twist from the other, twisting evenly and slowly as shown in Photo C, *page 140.* The rope will become thinner the more it is twisted. Press ropes on pot.

5 For dots, roll clay into round balls and press onto clay.

6 After the flowerpot is covered with clay, bake it according to the clay manufacturer's instructions. Let cool. If needed, glue loosened clay pieces to the flowerpot.

Gilded Terra-Cotta Pots

Brush a little paint on flowerpots and saucers to make them sparkling beauties.

 Clay Flowerpots
- 2½- and 4-inch-high terra-cotta flowerpots and 3- and 4-inch-wide saucers

 Acrylic Paints
- tan, metallic gold, and metallic red

 Basic Supplies
- paintbrush
- thick white crafts glue

Here's how

1 Paint the outside of each saucer tan. Paint the outside of the flowerpots tan below the rim. Paint the flowerpot rims metallic gold. Let the paint dry.

2 On each flowerpot, paint irregular streaks of metallic red from the bottom up onto the sides. Paint a metallic red stripe around each saucer. Let the paint dry.

3 Use a small paintbrush and metallic red and tan paint to make a decorative floral pattern around the gold rim using the patterns, *below*, for inspiration.

4 Use glue to attach the base of the saucer to the base of the pot. Let the glue dry.

Floral Patterns

Funky 'n' Fun

Accent bold designs with gold to make striking holders for your blooms.

 Clay Flowerpots
- desired size

 Polymer Clay
- colors to coordinate with paints

 Acrylic Paints
- lavender, yellow, orange, light blue, or other desired colors

 Marking Pens
- metallic gold

 Basic Supplies
- tracing paper
- pencil
- transfer paper
- paintbrush
- glass baking dish
- strong glue, such as E6000 (optional)

Here's how

1 Using the photo, *right,* and the patterns, *page 149,* plan the flowerpot design. To separate sections of color, use wavy lines, scallops, or stripes.

2 Trace the desired designs, *page 149.* Use transfer paper to transfer the designs to the flowerpot.

3 Paint the outlined sections of the flowerpot with acrylic paint. Let the paint dry.

4 Use gold marking pen to outline designs and add smaller motifs on the blocks of color as shown on *page 148.*

5 For flowerpot feel, roll four grape-size balls from clay. Flatten slightly and place on a glass baking dish. Bake in the oven according to the clay manufacturer's directions. Let cool. Glue to the bottom of the flowerpot. Let dry.

continued on page 148

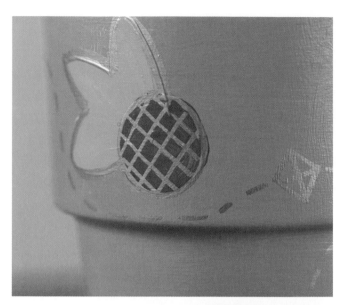

Abstract Flowers

Use the patterns, *opposite,* to make these interesting shapes. For a more realistic look, omit the gold lines on the orange and add green leaves to the design.

Checked Circles

To create this circular design in additional sizes, trace around round objects, such as lids or drinking glasses. Use a ruler to draw the straight lines.

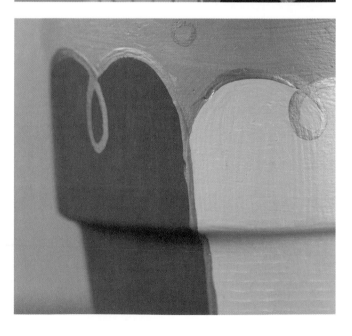

Curly Scallop

Section off large areas of color using this ornate edge. For other designs draw them on paper before transferring to the flowerpot.

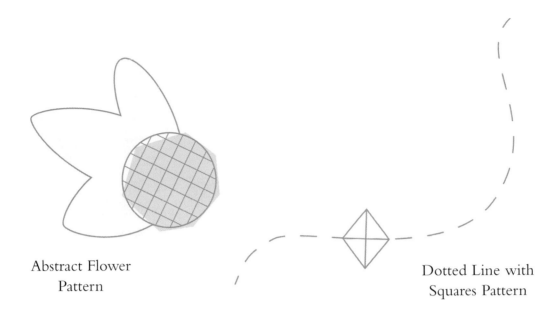

Abstract Flower
Pattern

Dotted Line with
Squares Pattern

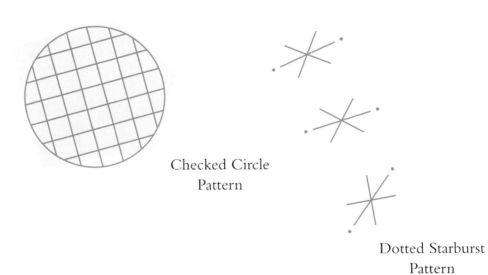

Checked Circle
Pattern

Dotted Starburst
Pattern

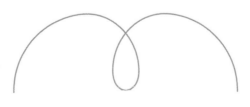

Curly Scallop
Pattern

All Swirled Up

Clay coils dance on this painted flowerpot that's just the right size to keep hair accessories at hand.

Clay Flowerpots
• desired size

Polymer Clay
• yellow, teal, and purple

Acrylic Paints
• maroon

Basic Supplies
• paintbrush
• scissors
• thick white
  crafts glue (optional)
• glass baking dish

Here's how

1 Paint the flowerpot. Let dry.

2 To make swirls, roll several clay coils from each clay color. Shape the coils as desired and press onto the surface of the flowerpot. Use the side of scissors to make indentations along each shape.

3 Bake the clay-covered pot in the oven according to the manufacturer's directions, not exceeding 235° F. Let cool.

4 If needed, glue loosened clay pieces to the flowerpot.

Funky Flowerpot Box

Create a colorful clay lid to top a painted terra-cotta flowerpot.

Here's how

1 Use half a package of polymer clay and roll to a ¼-inch-thick circle larger than the top of the flowerpot. Center and press the top of the pot into the clay to create an indentation. Cut away excess clay ¼ inch beyond impression. Remove pot and turn lid over; smooth out the edge of the lid.

2 Roll a thin rope of clay in a contrasting color. Place the rope around the top edge of the lid. Use the edge of a toothpick to press the rope into the lid at regular intervals.

3 Roll small balls of clay and flatten to make polka dots. Make enough to place on the lid, just inside the rope edge.

4 Roll a 6-inch-long thin clay rope and shape it into a spiral; leave one tail end up in a hook shape for the knob. Keep the knob separate from the lid until after baking.

5 On a baking dish, bake the lid and knob according to the clay manufacturer's directions. Let cool. Glue the knob to the center of the lid.

6 Paint the flowerpot using colors that coordinate with the lid. Let the paint dry.

Clay Flowerpots
• small

Polymer Clay
• desired colors

Acrylic Paints
• desired colors

+ Basic Supplies
• rolling pin
• crafts knife
• toothpick
• glass baking dish
• thick white crafts glue
• paintbrush

151

Pillars on Pillars

Stack terra-cotta saucers on upside-down flowerpots to create playful candleholders.

 Clay Flowerpots
- desired size with saucer to fit on top

 Polymer Clay
- red, white, and black

 Acrylic Paints
- black and red

 Basic Supplies
- paintbrush
- rolling pin
- scissors
- thick white crafts glue
- glass baking dish

Here's how

1 Paint the flowerpot and the saucer the desired colors. Let the paint dry.

2 To make large circles, knead a grape-size pieces of clay into a smooth, soft consistency. Roll into balls and press onto the rim. Roll pea-size balls from contrasting clay and press in the centers and on the flowerpot.

3 To make ropes, twist two clay coils together to form a striped rope to trim an edge.

4 For triangles, roll out clay into ⅛-inch-thick pieces and cut into triangular shapes. Shape over the edges of the saucers as shown in the photo, *opposite*.

5 Bake the flowerpot and saucer in the oven according to the clay manufacturer's instructions, not exceeding 235° F. Let cool.

6 Glue clay pieces to pots if they are not adhered. Glue saucer bottom to flowerpot bottom. Let the glue dry before using.

Polka-Dot Pot

Create a band of interest by pressing clay balls around the brim of a flowerpot.

 Clay Flowerpots
- tall and slender

 Polymer Clay
- 4 desired colors

 Acrylic Paints
- desired colors

+ Basic Supplies
- water
- paintbrush
- sequins (optional)
- thick white crafts glue (optional)
- glass baking dish

Here's how

1 Thin paint with water. Using a fairly dry brush, paint the flowerpot, allowing the brush marks to be visible. Paint the rim a contrasting color if desired. Let dry.

2 Roll balls of polymer clay into various sizes using four colors. Place clay balls, one at a time, spacing them apart on the top outer edge of the flowerpot. Press the balls flat using your thumb.

3 Bake the flowerpot in the oven according to the clay manufacturer's instructions, not exceeding 235° F. Let cool.

4 Glue small sequins by the clay polka dots if desired. Let the glue dry.

index

glossary

Acrylic Paint
A water-based, quick-drying paint that cleans up with soap and water. Some are developed for outdoor use while others are for interior use only.

Air-Dry Clay
Lightweight clay, available in white and colors, that dries without baking in the oven. The clay is paintable when dry. A common brand is Crayola Model Magic.

Base Coat
A first coat of paint that is used to prepare a surface for more paint or to provide a background color.

Cardstock
Heavy solid-color paper available in large sheets in art stores and small sheets in scrapbooking stores.

Colored Wire
Available in different thicknesses, this wire is available in metallic colors and plastic-coated for more matte finishes.

Craft Foam
This foam is available in varying weight sheets and many colors. It can also be purchased in pre-cut shapes and letters.

Elastic Cord
This cord is available in colors and clear. There are a variety of types of elastic used in sewing and jewelry making. The type used for some of the projects in this book are clear or colored jewelry elastic cord.

Fringe
A border or trim of cords or threads, hanging loose or tied in bunches. Fringe on paper is made with close narrow cuts to give the appearance of a fringed edge.

Glass Paints
These paints can be acrylic (water-based) or enamel (oil-based). Some glass paints require the painted object to be baked in the oven for the paint to become permanent.

Ink Pad
A boxed pad saturated with ink. The pads are used with rubber stamps to transfer designs. The ink is available in a rainbow of solid colors, mixed colors, and metallics.

Iridescent
Often used when referring to paint, iridescent colors change when seen from different angles.

Knead

To press and mix together.

Marking Pens

These pens come in a variety of colors, including metallics, and have a range of tip sizes. Many will soak through surfaces such as paper, so protect your work surface with layers of newspaper if necessary.

Polymer Clay

An easy-to-mold clay that becomes hard and permanently shaped when baked in the oven. Common brands are Sculpey, Fimo, and Premo.

Rolling Pin

A wood or plastic kitchen tool, used to roll out dough, that can be used to flatten clay.

Rubber Stamps

A block, usually wood, that has a rubber design on one side. To stamp, the rubber surface is pressed onto an ink pad and then pressed on a surface to transfer the design.

Scrapbook Papers

Solid, print, and textured papers created specifically for

scrapbooking and cardmaking. Common sizes are 12-inch squares and 8½×11 inches. These papers are available in scrapbooking, crafts, stamping, and discount stores.

Seed Beads

Small round glass beads often used in jewelry making. The beads are available in a variety of sizes and colors.

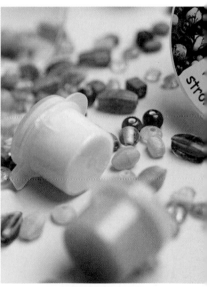

Texture

The appearance or feel of a surface.

Trace

Drawing around an object or copying the lines of drawn art.

Tracing Paper

A thin sheet of semi-transparent paper used to copy drawings or patterns.

Tube Bead

A small glass bead that is a long, narrow shape.

sources

Adhesives
Aleenes
duncancrafts.com

Centis
Centis Consumer Products
Division
888/236-8476

Elmer's Glue Stick
800/848-9400
elmers.com
comments@elmers.com

Suze Weinberg Design Studio
732/761-2400
732/761-2410 (fax)
Suzenj@aol.com

Tombow USA
800/835-3232
tombowusa.com

Buttons
Le Bouton Buttons
Blumenthal Lansing Co.
563/538-4211
563/538-4243 (fax)
sales@buttonsplus.com

Foam Squares
Therm O Web
800/323-0799

Rubber Stamps/Ink Pads
Art Impressions
800/393-2014
artimpressions.com

Stampin' Up!
801/601-5400
stampinup.com

Scissors, Punches & Rounders
Creative Memories
800/341-5275
creativememories.com

Fiskars Scissors
608/259-1649
fiskars.com

Emagination Crafts, Inc.
866/238-9770
service@emaginationcraftsinc
.com

EK Success Ltd.
eksuccess.com
(Wholesale only. Available at most crafts stores.)

Scrapbook Papers
All My Memories
888/553-1998

Anna Griffin
404/817-8170
404/817-0590 (fax)
annagriffin.com

Art Accents
360/733-8989
artaccents.net

Bazzill Basics Paper
480/558-8557
bazzillbasics.com

Colorbök
800/366-4660
colorbok.com

Daisy D's Paper Co.
801/447-8955
daisydspaper.com

DMD, Inc.
800/805-9890

Doodlebug
801/966-9952

Family Archives
888/622-6556
heritagescrapbooks.com

Frances Meyer, Inc.
800/372-6237
francesmeyer.com

Hot Off The Press, Inc.
800/227-9595
paperpizazz.com

Karen Foster Design, Inc.
karenfosterdesign.com

Making Memories
800/286-5263
makingmemories.com

Memories Forever
Westrim Crafts
800/727-2727
westrimcrafts.com

The Paper Loft
866/254-1961 (toll free)
paperloft.com
(Wholesale only. Available at most crafts stores.)

Pixie Press
888/834-2883
pixiepress.com

Plaid Enterprises, Inc.
800/842-4197
plaidonline.com

Provo Craft
provocraft.com
(Wholesale only. Available at most crafts stores.)

Sandylion
800/387-4215
905/475-0523
(International)
sandylion.com

Scrap-ease What's New, Ltd.
800/272-3874
480/832-2928 (fax)
whatsnewltd.com

Sweetwater
14711 Road 15
Fort Morgan, CO 80701
970/867-4428

Westrim Crafts
800/727-2727

Wübie Prints
wubieprints.com
(Wholesale only. Available at most crafts stores.)

Two Busy Moms
800/272-4794
TwoBusyMoms.com

Stickers
Canson
800/628-9283
canson-us.com

The Gifted Line
John Grossman, Inc.
310/390-9900

Highsmith
800/558-3899
highsmith.com

K & Co.
816/389-4150
KandCompany.com

me & my BIG ideas
949/589-4607
meandmybigideas.com

Mrs. Grossman's Paper Co.
800/429-4549
mrsgrossmans.com

Once Upon A Scribble
702/896-2181
onceuponascribble.com

Paper Punch
800/397-2737

Paper House Productions
800/255-7316
paperhouseproductions.com

SRM Press
800/323-9589
srmpress.com
(Wholesale only. Available at most crafts stores.)

Stickopotamus
P.O. Box 1047
Clifton, NJ 07014-1047
973/594-0540 (fax)
stickopotamus.com

Paints
Angelwings–Radiant Pearls
3322 West Sussix Way
Fresno, CA 93722
800/400-3717
radiantpearls.com

Createx Colors
14 Airport Park Road
East Granby, CT 06026
800/243-2712

DecoArt
Highway 150 & 27
Stanford, KY 40484
800/367-3047
decoart.com

Design Master Color Tool, Inc.
P.O. Box 601
Boulder, CO 80306
303/443-5214
dmcolor.com

J.W. etc.
2205 First Street, Suite 103
Simi Valley, CA 93065
805/526-5066 (voice mail)
805/526-1297 (fax)
jwetc.com

Krylon Products Group
Cleveland, OH 44115
800/797-3332
krylon.com

McCloskey Special Effects
Division of Valspur Corp.
800/345-4530

Plaid Enterprises, Inc.
800/842-4197
678/291-8100
plaidonline.com

The Testor Corporation
440 Blackhawk Park Avenue
Rockford, IL 61104
800/962-6654